Fault Detection in Microservice Architectures

Integrating Software Fault Prediction with DevSecOps

Deepak Sharma
Aamiruddin Syed

Apress®

Fault Detection in Microservice Architectures: Integrating Software Fault Prediction with DevSecOps

Deepak Sharma
New Delhi, Delhi, India

Aamiruddin Syed
New Delhi, Delhi, India

ISBN-13 (pbk): 979-8-8688-2711-2
https://doi.org/10.1007/979-8-8688-2712-9

ISBN-13 (electronic): 979-8-8688-2712-9

Managing Director, Apress Media LLC: Welmoed Spahr
Acquisitions Editor: Anandadeep Roy
Coordinating Editor: Jessica Vakili
Copy Editor: Kezia Endsley

Cover image by Pixabay.com

Distributed to the book trade worldwide by Springer Science+Business Media New York, 1 New York Plaza, New York, NY 10004. Phone 1-800-SPRINGER, fax (201) 348-4505, e-mail orders-ny@springer-sbm.com, or visit www.springeronline.com. Apress Media, LLC is a Delaware LLC and the sole member (owner) is Springer Science + Business Media Finance Inc (SSBM Finance Inc). SSBM Finance Inc is a Delaware corporation.

For information on translations, please e-mail booktranslations@springernature.com; for reprint, paperback, or audio rights, please e-mail bookpermissions@springernature.com.

Apress titles may be purchased in bulk for academic, corporate, or promotional use. eBook versions and licenses are also available for most titles. For more information, reference our Print and eBook Bulk Sales web page at http://www.apress.com/bulk-sales.

Any source code or other supplementary material referenced by the author in this book is available to readers on GitHub (https://github.com/Apress). For more detailed information, please visit https://www.apress.com/gp/services/source-code.

If disposing of this product, please recycle the paper

To our lovely parents

Table of Contents

About the Authors

Deepak Sharma is associate director at the School of Open Learning, University of Delhi, and a seasoned researcher in software engineering and fault prediction, with over a decade of experience. He holds a Ph.D. in computer science and multiple advanced degrees in technology and applications. His academic work focuses on software quality improvement, defect prediction models, and statistical analysis of software metrics. He has published extensively in international journals and conferences and has been recognized by several government bodies for his research contributions.

Aamiruddin Syed is Cybersecurity expert and DevSecOps practitioner with deep expertise in secure software development, cloud-native architectures, and supply chain security. He has led DevSecOps implementations across global enterprises, integrating predictive risk models into CI/CD pipelines and Kubernetes-based environments.

Aamiruddin is the author of *Supply Chain Software Security: AI, IoT, and Application Security* (Apress, 2024) and a frequent speaker at DEFCON, Black Hat MEA, RSA and other international cybersecurity forums. His insights ensure that the book translates rigorous models into actionable, real-world strategies for developers, security engineers, and SRE teams.

About the Technical Reviewer

Kapil Sharma is a professor at the department of information technology, Delhi Technological University (formerly Delhi College of Engineering), Delhi, India. He holds a Ph.D. in computer science and engineering from the faculty of engineering and technology at the M. D. University, Rohtak (Haryana), India. He obtained a bachelor's degree in engineering and a master's degree in computer science and engineering and information technology. His research interests include system design, pattern recognition, computer vision, and soft computing. He has published more than 100 research papers in referred journals and conferences. He is an IEEE Transactions, Elsevier, Springer, and Taylor & Francis journal reviewer.

Acknowledgments

It is with immense joy that we acknowledge the support of our parents, who always encouraged us with all their patience and experience.

We owe our heartfelt thanks to our friends, for all their valuable input throughout this work.

Our sincere thanks goes out to the Apress team, for allowing us to pursue this work with great enthusiasm. And a special thanks to the reviewers as well.

Finally, this journey is placed at the holy feet of the almighty.

With Gratitude to the Existence.

Introduction

The quick transition to cloud-native computing has resulted in the adoption of microservice architectures, whereby applications are made up of loosely coupled, independently deployable services that improve scalability and responsiveness at the cost of much more complicated systems. This distributed aspect poses a challenge related to propagation of faults. Analyzing root causes becomes difficult as well. This makes the conventional fault-detection techniques inadequate. Simultaneously, DevSecOps is a radical paradigm that unites development, security, and operations into continuous integration and deployment pipelines, which allows vulnerabilities to be detected early and the system to be ensured at all times throughout the software lifecycle.

The book addresses how software fault-prediction methods can be combined with DevSecOps practices to provide proactive, intelligent, and scalable fault detection in a microservice setting. It explains how to use advances in machine learning, anomaly detectors, and observability to construct resilient and secure systems that adapt to the changing operational and threat environment.

PART I

Foundations

CHAPTER 1

Introduction to Software Fault Prediction in DevSecOps

1.1 Overview of Software Faults

Software is being developed at incredible speeds. It is not unusual for a developer to write code and then be testing and deploying it in mere hours. Agile teams release new features into production almost daily. Complex systems of microservices communicate with one another.

Automated security tests run in the background. Consumers expect instant reliability in the critical software tools that they use. Companies have no option other than to operate flawlessly. Finding faults early also allows for more targeted manual regression testing so that QA tests perform with maximum impact and minimum cost, rather than finding bugs after a release.

At its most basic, software fault prediction is an approach that tries to determine quantitatively which parts of a software system are more likely to fail or be defective. These faults might not yet have manifested as bugs in the software in production, but similar code has been found to cause problems in the past under particular conditions. Like weather forecasting for your codebase, just as meteorologists look at past weather patterns for their predictions, engineers look at past defect patterns. Some experts agree that the best time to predict potential software defects is before software testing begins—the earlier in the software lifecycle the prediction occurs the better. As well as increasing software quality, predicting faults promotes more accurate cost-escalation fixes and

D. Sharma and A. Syed, *Fault Detection in Microservice Architectures*,
https://doi.org/10.1007/979-8-8688-2712-9_1

ensures that reliable software is delivered on time. In particular, making a forecast in the coding phase of the SDLC (software development lifecycle) can classify which modules might be fault-prone and thus align the optimum fixes. Software is difficult to make error-free due to the complexity of modern systems, limits of human cognition, and limits of time/resources for developing software. Methods of software defect prediction factor metrics that are derived from code architecture are commonly used for this purpose. Those methods are based on the principle that more complex areas in architecture are more susceptible to faults in the code. Structural metrics (quantitative measures of different aspects of code complexity) can sometimes be used to build a prediction model. To the extent that the various metrics that are used comprise different aspects of code complexity, they are not completely independent. Factor analysis is a way of uncovering some of these latent variables, or underlying factors, that synthesize the metrics into independent factors that predict code complexity.

This book proposes a linear regression model of fault prediction based on these latent variables. Various forms of factorization of data are described, and it is known that these can be beneficial in some cases for tissue prediction. However, latent variable interactions remain, for the most part, unexplored. This book attempts to bridge this gap with research studying latent variable interactions. Now imagine you lead a DevSecOps team in charge of a microservice architecture that has highly automated everything and monitors everything. It's finally time to review your code and do a smooth deployment! And all is perfect, until three days later when users start getting some random login errors. Nothing failed during testing and nothing showed up in your CI/CD pipeline. But something is wrong—something lying in wait deep in the service, almost hidden in plain sight.

After hours of searching, digging into the code bit by bit, the team uncovers a logic error, something that had managed to fly beneath the radar. The result of this simple mistake was terrible. Could they have avoided it? It happens that they could, which is where security frameworks and practices (SFP) come in. Fault prediction is not only about keeping track of bugs, but also about utilizing the power of anticipation and knowing where the code is most likely to go awry, even before the first line has been coded. Fluently incorporated into the DevSecOps methodology, SFP redefines the concept of quality in connection with security, user experience, and the stability of operations. This book explores the inner workings of fault prediction, from the reasons why it is important, to the ways in which SFP can be integrated into state-of-the-art microservice architecture. Central to this are the techniques, measures, and contents underpinning it, including how SFP can assist siloed developers in constructing more intelligently and assist teams in producing smarter and safer systems. We are in an age and era where software is always on. It is no longer an option to be reactive—it is time to predict the faults before they become failures.

Figure 1-1 illustrates the workflow of fault prediction within a DevSecOps environment. The SFP process in a DevSecOps system begins with the code commit and code review, followed by the automated AI model analysis of the code to identify the likely faults. Reports and predictions are forwarded to the devs for fixes, and to security analysts to enable early detection and mitigation and compliance checks. When the system is validated, the CI/CD pipeline triggers deployment and the monitoring tools start giving feedback on live performance. That phase directs the loop toward gathering data to improve. During the next release, more timely bug fixes come on board, and quality and security improve.

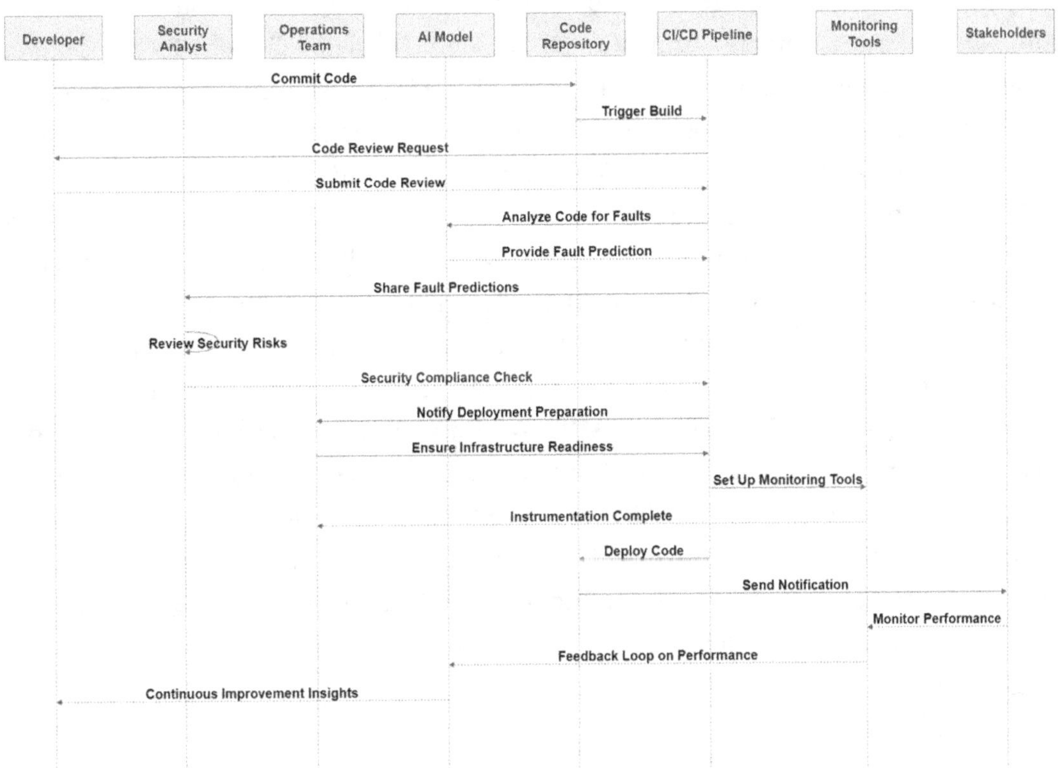

Figure 1-1. *Integration of software fault prediction in the DevSecOps pipeline*

1.2 Why Fault Prediction Is Vital in DevSecOps

We will never create perfect software, nor will the vast majority of software fail in production. Even moderately-sized applications consist of millions of lines of code and the number of potential execution paths that we need to test vastly exceeds the exams that we have time to write and run. What the people who create the software are left to do is test where they think it is most likely to be "broken"—a word similar to the German aspect of "bug" here. Software fault prediction (SFP) is the buggy-math that captures and analyzes historical data relating to software bugs and uses that data (and other code metrics) and predictive models to indicate which modules, classes, or functions are more likely to be buggy. By doing this, the QAs know what/where to start targeted combing testing and are able to accomplish the tasks faster and make better use of their time.

A quite smaller percentage of the code segment responsible for the bulk of those failures, as always, is depicted using the "80/20" Pareto principle. When SFP helps target these methods, regression testing can be focused on bigger issues before going into the far reaches of the software cave. DevSecOps has touched every team and here they are doing big data triage on security. This places security and quality assurance firmly within the software development lifecycle as it is happening, not after the fact. In today's DevSecOps pipeline, where a change in code is automatically continuously integrated (CI), tested, and continuously deployed (CD) on shared code branches, the ability to foresee and stop a software fault as an early warning in the code development is more critical than ever. With faults predicted in modules, defects can be identified before they happen during the initial stages of the SDLC—during coding, commit, and build. Getting an early warning about a module that is likely to cause problems helps dev teams spot defects before they escalate. This is better aligned with today's DevSecOps "shift left" method of moving testing and review of security validation earlier up the SDLC timeline (period of time between the request for proposal [RFP] and system release) from the cost-avoidance necessity to lower risk downstream.

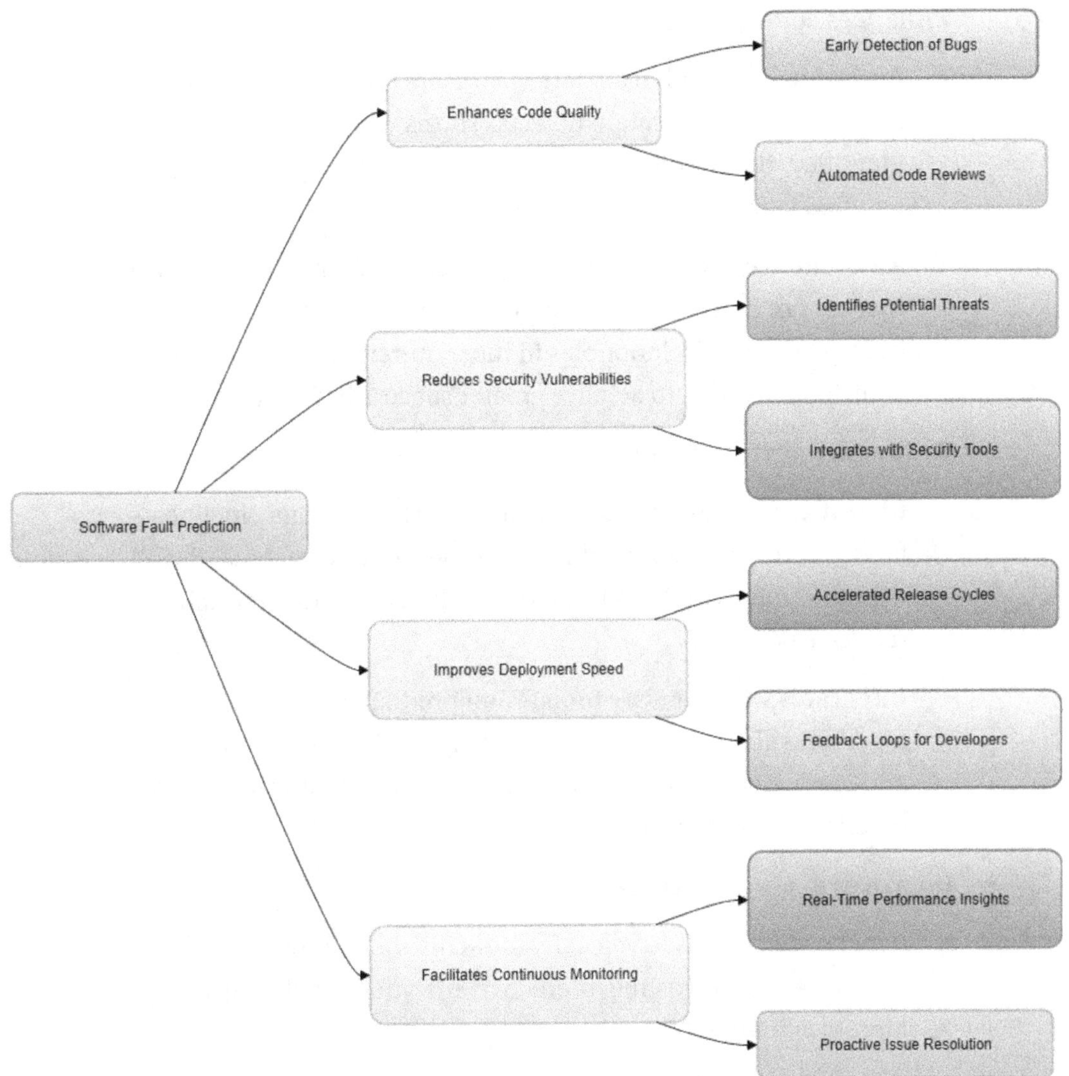

Figure 1-2. *Key benefits of software fault prediction in DevSecOps*

Figure 1-2 identifies the key benefits of software fault prediction as part of a DevSecOps pipeline. Fault prediction not only detects the possible defects beforehand, but also enhances security, deployment, and maintenance of constant monitoring of applications. Every branch depicts how predictive analytics can be used in the contemporary practice of software engineering:

1. **Enhances code quality**
    - **Early detection of bugs:** Models indicate points that contain or are probable to contain defects. The earlier the defect is identified, the simpler and less costly it is to rectify (unless it is rectified before it gets to the production stage).
    - **Automated code reviews:** AI code checkers eliminate unknowns that are not detected by automatically analyzing the source code. They identify loopholes in the requirements or design that contribute to fault, to achieve greater success in final test.
2. **Reduces security vulnerabilities**
    - **Identifies potential threats:** Used in the DevSecOps pipeline, fault prediction is compatible with tools of static analysis (SAST), dynamic analysis (DAST), and dependency scanning, which reduce risk.
    - **Integrates with security tools:** Fault prediction can be used together with static analysis (SAST), dynamic analysis (DAST), and dependency scanner tools by integrating it into DevSecOps pipelines to address risks.
3. **Improves deployment speed**
    - **Accelerated release cycles:** By reducing the number of faults discovered late in testing, predictive analytics enables faster and more confident releases.
    - **Feedback loops for developers:** Developers receive real-time feedback on fault-prone areas, allowing them to address issues immediately and maintain velocity.
4. **Facilitates continuous monitoring**
    - **Real-time performance insights:** Integrated with monitoring tools, fault prediction continues to provide valuable runtime insights to teams, helping them avoid performance bottlenecks before they arise.

DevSecOps is characterized by close integration, continuous monitoring, and security. It's automated, secure, and fast. We can no longer wait for manual testing after a deployment. Everything is automated.

CI/CD is table stakes now, and so is built-in security. We need to manage vulnerabilities during development, not reach for that burning fuse late in the sprint. Our systems are now microservices comprised of hundreds of small, loosely coupled services and we've lost track of the dependencies. Fault prediction offers a single monitoring tool feature, one that warns of likely faulty modules before we deploy.

1.2.1 Example: Microservice Deployment Scenario

Consider a microservice company that deploys 20 microservices a day. Keeping that in mind, picture a service running in one of those containers. Let's say it handles a credit score request from a user. If that service goes down, they lose their services and/or the loan. With fault prediction as part of the DevSecOps pipeline, devs are warned that this one service is likely to fail due to cyclomatic complexity and are told how often it's being changed. This can stop a sinking production sail away from the dock.

1.3 Components and Process of Fault Prediction

Figure 1-1 walks through a fault-prediction workflow in the context of a DevSecOps pipeline. After code has been committed and reviewed, it's passed off to an AI analyst to predict the most fault-prone parts. Then we hand it over to our software developers and security analysts so that they can examine risks found and ensure compliance. Then we do a CI/CD roll out and provide continuous feedback. That completes the loop. Not only does this build better software, but it also helps us do this more securely and live by the precepts of continuous improvement outlined previously.

The fault prediction process typically involves two major stages:

1. **Identifying fault-prone modules**

   Predictive models leverage historical defect data and software metrics to classify modules as fault-prone or not. Key metrics include code complexity, change frequency, coupling, cohesion, and module size, among others.

2. **Isolating and mitigating faults**

   Once fault-prone modules are identified, efforts focus on addressing these areas. This may involve conducting more rigorous testing, refactoring problematic code, or strengthening integration points that influence other modules.

Once identified, fault-prone modules are prioritized for mitigation. Strategies include intensified testing, code refactoring, or reinforcing integration points to prevent defects from affecting interconnected components.

Since a small subset of components typically accounts for most defects, focusing quality assurance (QA) efforts on these modules optimizes resource allocation. Identifying modules with system-wide influence is critical, as defects in these areas can trigger cascading failures.

Fault prediction relies on software metrics such as:

- **Size metrics:** Lines of code (LOC), number of classes, and functions.
- **Complexity metrics:** Cyclomatic complexity, control-flow structures, and depth of inheritance.
- **Coupling and cohesion metrics:** Interdependencies between modules and the internal consistency of classes.
- **Change metrics:** Frequency of modifications, churn, and commit history.

The underlying assumption is that code regions with higher structural complexity are more error-prone. However, these metrics are often correlated and not statistically independent, which complicates predictive modeling. Machine learning and statistical models are trained on these metrics and historical defect data in order to detect patterns distinguishing fault-prone modules from stable ones.

This book uses a new technique, called *factor analysis with linear regression*. It groups the metrics in latent variables and reduces redundancy, aiding in finding any faults with greater precision.

1.4 Software Faults: An Inevitable Reality

Before diving deeper, this section clarifies what we mean by "faults." A software fault is a flaw in the source code that may lead to a failure at runtime. The type of flaws can vary widely from flawed logic to an off-by-one error to unhandled edge cases.

1.4.1 Real-World Example: Knight Capital Trading Glitch

In August of 2012, Knight Capital Group, a major Wall Street firm, experienced a trading glitch that resulted in a loss of $440 Million in just 45 minutes. The glitch occurred when a piece of old, unused code was accidentally re-enabled during a software upgrade. Once the system went live, it began executing thousands of unwanted stock trades per second. If fault predictions were being made, and if this unused code had been identified as high-risk in a DevSecOps pipeline with automated validation and static analysis, the glitch might have been avoided, and the losses associated with it avoided also.

1.4.2 GitHub Outage (2018)

In October of 2018, GitHub suffered a partial outage because of an unexpected failure in the company's database replication system caused by a scheduled maintenance operation. The outage was the result of an unforeseen response by the failover mechanism in the database replication system. This is a good example of a latent software fault revealing itself under the stress of a normal maintenance operation. If GitHub had been utilizing predictive models that simulate historical failure modes and assess infrastructure preparedness, this outage may have been avoided.

1.5 Where Fault Prediction Fits in the SDLC and DevSecOps

Historically, fault prediction was considered to be a quality assurance function performed during testing. However, as organizations move toward implementing DevSecOps methodologies and practices, quality assurance functions are now expected to take place as soon as possible (to be moved to the left).

Here's how fault prediction integrates into DevSecOps:

Stage	Role of Fault Prediction
Plan	Identify high-risk modules from historical data to prioritize design attention
Develop	Alert developers during coding about risky modules (e.g., via IDE plugins)
Build/Test	Use predictive models to guide unit and integration testing focus
Release	Gate releases based on fault risk scores for critical services
Monitor	Feed production fault data back into models for continuous improvement

1.6 From Metrics to Models: Factor Analysis Approach

While many studies have indicated the value of incorporating multiple metrics into defect prediction models, few studies have explored the interactions among latent variables and their cumulative effect on predictive analytics. Identifying the interactions among latent variables may reveal additional patterns and relationships that could improve the accuracy and reliability of predictive models used for fault prediction in DevSecOps environments.

As such, this book is positioned to contribute to the existing body of knowledge by providing an empirical assessment of the interactive effects of latent variables and the degree to which they affect predictive models developed for the purpose of predicting faults in software. The results of this book are expected to provide insights into the development of more accurate and reliable predictive models for use in DevSecOps environments.

1.6.1 Example

Let's say we have the following metrics for a module:

- LOC = 500
- Cyclomatic Complexity = 25
- Coupling Between Objects (CBO) = 12

Instead of feeding all three directly into a model, factor analysis may determine that these metrics belong to a single latent factor, called "Structural Complexity." The regression model then uses this factor, reducing dimensionality and improving interpretability.

1.7 Benefits of Early Fault Prediction in Microservices

The use of the microservices technology represents opportunities and challenges presented by software fault prediction.

1.7.1 Benefits

- **Targeted testing:** Allows prioritization of testing efforts for critical services.
- **Resource optimization:** Reduces unnecessary testing of stable modules.
- **Risk management:** Supports informed deployment strategies (e.g., canary releases for high-risk services).
- **Security enhancement:** Fault-prone code often correlates with security vulnerabilities.

1.7.2 Challenges

Achieving completely fault-free software remains highly challenging due to several factors:

- **System complexity:** Modern applications often include millions of lines of code, distributed systems, and interconnected services, all of which increase the likelihood of defects.
- **Human cognitive limitations:** Software development is a highly intricate intellectual activity, and errors can arise from misinterpretations of requirements, design oversights, or lapses in implementation.
- **Resource constraints:** Time, budget, and staffing limitations make it impossible to exhaustively test every possible execution path.

Due to the nature of these challenges, the objective shifts from finding and removing all faults to strategically managing and limiting the occurrence of faults using predictive methods and focused testing.

1.8 Case Study Snapshot: Predicting Faults in a DevSecOps Pipeline

For the purpose of illustration, historical data from five large software systems was used to analyze the relationship between CK (Chidamber and Kemerer) and OO (object-oriented) metrics. Using factor analysis, the predictive model improved on traditional linear models.

1.8.1 Insight

The model has discovered that a comparatively limited number of modules led to the majority of the past failures. This agrees with the Pareto principle (also known as the 80/20 rule), according to which 20 percent of the modules produce 80 percent of the problems.

This allowed the DevSecOps team to:

- Focus manual code reviews on the high-risk 20 percent
- Introduce automated static analysis tools specifically for those components
- Improve test case generation for fault-prone modules

1.9 Existing Literature and Gaps

Previous studies have also proved the advantages of combining various metrics and latent variables in predicting the defects. Nevertheless, there is no adequate research on which the latent variables interact and the net influence of such interactions on predictive analytics. Knowledge of the interactions of the latent variables is valuable, as it can help establish patterns and relationship that were previously unknown, which can enhance the accuracy and reliability of predictive models applied in fault prediction. This thesis is based on prior studies that examine the effects of interaction between latent variables through empirical investigation and evaluation of the implications of the interaction on models utilized to predict software faults. This provides outcomes that can be utilized to design stronger predictive models, which would be valuable in real-life DevSecOps settings.

1.10 Conclusion

Software fault prediction is no longer something a large corporation can afford not to do—it is a necessity of any organization that desires to offer reliable, secure, and maintainable software in a fast-paced DevSecOps environment. Fault prediction allows teams to target their testing and remediation energies where they will make the most positive contribution. This makes testing and remediation activities more efficient and effective. Besides that, fault prediction helps guarantee software quality, helps lower costs, and leads to faster delivery times. Teams can optimally apply testing and remediation to the most fault-prone areas. Fault prediction added to the pipelines of DevSecOps, as shown in Figure 1-1, contributes to the robustness of security and quality assurance throughout the development lifecycle.

The next chapter discusses how this predictive capability can be introduced into DevSecOps pipelines in specific microservice-based architectures, with modularity and complexity meeting. That chapter examines prediction models, evaluation criteria, integration options, and examples of use in practice.

CHAPTER 2

Statistical Foundations for Fault Detection

Software engineers have been asking themselves the same question for nearly a century: What parts of our code are likely to break? Having the answer to this question is no longer optional—it's becoming increasingly imperative due to DevSecOps' emphasis on speed, automation, and security. Today's complex software systems rely on a wide variety of components, including cloud-based services, mobile apps, web portals, IoT devices, and much more. Because of this, a single flaw or error in one component could potentially impact thousands of other components or even entire systems. Furthermore, the cost associated with identifying and repairing errors late in the development cycle is significantly greater than the cost of addressing them early. As a result, the primary objective of software engineers is to find faults before they cause problems. To accomplish this goal, software engineers utilize a variety of statistical methodologies that enable them to measure and evaluate the quality of their source code.

This chapter discusses the statistical methodology employed in software fault detection. More specifically, it describes the use of linear regression and multiple regression as well as factor analysis in detecting faults in software applications. These statistical methodologies are utilized to identify relationships between various characteristics of software applications and the propensity of those applications to develop faults. Once a relationship has been established, software engineers can utilize the statistical models developed to forecast which software applications are more likely to develop faults and thus take corrective action prior to the occurrence of the faults.

D. Sharma and A. Syed, *Fault Detection in Microservice Architectures*,
https://doi.org/10.1007/979-8-8688-2712-9_2

2.1 The Role of Statistics in Fault Detection

Every software system carries risk, but not every line of code carries it equally. For example:

- A payment-processing microservice in a fintech app may have fewer lines of code than a reporting dashboard, but its coupling with external systems makes it more fault-prone.
- In an IoT system, firmware modules handling device updates may have a high density of defects compared to user-facing modules, because of their complexity and low testability.
- A telecommunications switch, as shown in studies from the 1990s, may contain millions of lines of code, but failure is repeatedly traced back to a small set of deeply nested functions.

These illustrations highlight one major observation—faults are patterned. Identifying those patterns is not possible without mathematical models that quantify the correlation between software metrics and defect probability. Here, statistical foundations cannot be ignored.

Once the statistical models have been created, software engineers can utilize the models to flag software applications that are likely to develop faults so that corrective action can be taken to prevent the faults from occurring. In addition, the statistical models developed during the software fault-detection process can be utilized to help identify the causes of faults and to assist in developing corrective actions to eliminate the causes of faults.

In this respect, three core statistical methods form the analytical backbone:

- Simple linear regression (LR)
- Multiple linear regression (MLR)
- Factor analysis with regression

Each plays a specific role in modeling, interpreting, and predicting software defects.

2.1.1 Simple Linear Regression (LR)

The simplest way to model fault-proneness is to examine the relationship between one software metric and the number of defects. This is done using linear regression (LR).

Formula

$$Y = \beta 0 + \beta 1 X + \epsilon$$

Where:

- Y = Dependent variable (e.g., the number of faults in a module)
- X = Independent variable (e.g., the lines of code)
- β0 = Intercept
- β1= Slope or weight of XXX
- ε = Error term (any variance not explained by the model)

Example

Consider two modules:

- Module A has 200 lines of code (LOC) and three known faults.
- Module B has 800 LOC and 12 known faults.

The simple linear regression model may indicate that the faults linearly depend on size. This is intuitive—the bigger the module, the more complicated it is and, thus, the more chance to make errors.

But software quality is rarely influenced by a single metric. Code complexity, coupling, and cohesion all interact to determine reliability. That leads us to multiple linear regression (MLR).

2.1.2 Multiple Linear Regression (MLR)

In practice, fault-proneness is influenced by multiple factors simultaneously—code complexity, cohesion, coupling, inheritance, and more. MLR generalizes the linear model to include multiple independent variables.

Mathematical Form

$$Y=\beta 0+\beta 1X1+\beta 2X2+\ldots+\beta nXn+\varepsilon$$

Where X1,X2,...,Xn represent different metrics such as:

- WMC (weighted methods per class)
- DIT (depth of inheritance tree)
- CBO (coupling between objects)

Example

Imagine we are analyzing a Java class with these metrics:

- WMC = 25
- CBO = 12
- DIT = 5

The regression model might look like this:

$$Faults=\beta 0+\beta 1\cdot 25+\beta 2\cdot 12+\beta 3\cdot 5+\varepsilon$$

If β2 (the weight for CBO) is very high, this indicates high coupling, which is a stronger predictor of faults than complexity alone.

Limitations

MLR assumes:

- No multicollinearity (independent variables should not be highly correlated)
- Linear relationship between inputs and output
- Homoscedasticity (constant variance of error terms)

However, software metrics (e.g., LOC and WMC) are often intercorrelated, which can distort the model. That's where factor analysis comes in.

2.1.3 Factor Analysis: Identifying Latent Variables

Factor analysis is another type of statistical methodology that is frequently employed in software fault detection. The primary reason for utilizing factor analysis is to identify the underlying structure of the data collected from software applications. When conducting a study on the quality of software applications, it is common for the software engineer to collect numerous types of data, such as the number of lines of code in a module, the number of methods in the module, and the number of faults that occur in the module. However, the data collected may be highly correlated, making it difficult for the software engineer to determine which variables are contributing to the quality of the software application. Factor analysis is used to identify the underlying structure of the data, which is composed of the individual variables (such as lines of code and number of faults) and the common underlying factors (such as complexity and maintainability) that contribute to the quality of the software application. The statistical equation for factor analysis is as follows.

Mathematical Form

$$X_i=\lambda_{i1}F_1+\lambda_{i2}F_2+\ldots+\lambda_{im}F_m+\varepsilon_i$$

Where:

- XiX_iXi: Observed metric (e.g., LOC, WMC, LCOM)
- $F_1,F_2,\ldots,F_m$: Underlying factors
- λ_{ij}: Factor loadings (relationship strength between metric and factor)
- ε_i: Error or unique variance for each metric

Essentially, factor analysis transforms a large set of potentially correlated metrics into a smaller set of uncorrelated factors.

Steps in Factor Analysis

1. **Correlation matrix construction:** Compute correlations between all software metrics.
2. **Extraction of initial factors:** Using methods like principal component analysis (PCA) or maximum likelihood.

3. **Rotation (optional):** Techniques like Varimax simplify the interpretation by maximizing loadings on each factor.
4. **Selection of factors:** Based on Eigenvalues or explained variance.

Example

Suppose we analyze the following metrics:

- WMC, LOC, RFC → May load on Factor 1 (complexity)
- DIT, NOC → May load on Factor 2 (inheritance depth)
- CBO, LCOM → May load on Factor 3 (coupling & cohesion)

These three latent factors now summarize the core structure of the software. They are then used as inputs to regression models.

2.2 Combining Factor Analysis with Regression

Once the underlying structure of the data has been determined through factor analysis, the next step is to conduct a regression analysis to predict the quality of the software application. This approach improves model interpretability and handles multicollinearity effectively. Figure 2-1 illustrates the complete methodological pipeline, starting from raw data collection and preparation, moving through exploratory and confirmatory factor analysis, and culminating in regression analysis and interpretation of results. The rationale behind using these factors as independent variables is that they represent the underlying structure of the data, and thus will be less prone to multicollinearity, which is a major limitation of multiple linear regression. The statistical equation for combining factor analysis with regression follows.

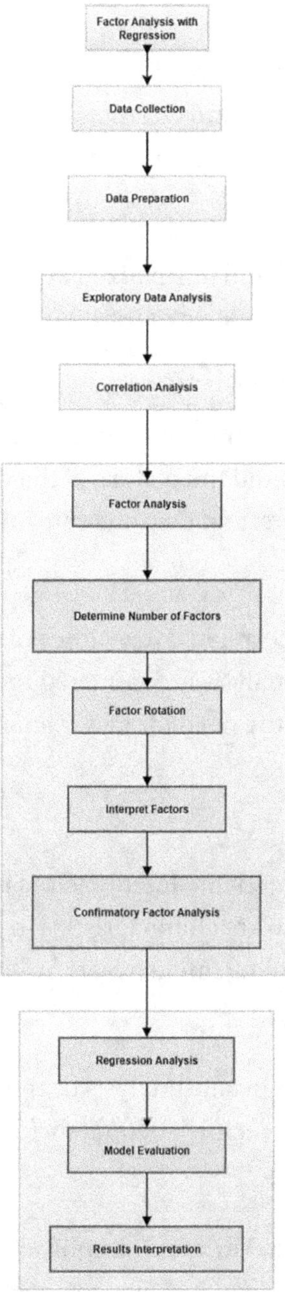

Figure 2-1. *Workflow of factor analysis with regression for fault prediction*

Figure 2-1 represents the structured workflow for applying factor analysis with regression in software fault prediction. Each step plays a crucial role in transforming raw software metrics into meaningful insights:

1. **Data Collection**

   Software repositories are sampled with metrics, including CK (Chidamber and Kemerer) and OO metrics (Examples: Weighted methods per class [WMC], coupling between objects [CBO], etc.).

2. **Data Preparation**

   Raw data is pre-cleaned and normalized and missing values are dealt with before the statistical analysis.

3. **Exploratory Data Analysis (EDA)**

   Certain basic statistical summaries and visualizations are conducted in order to build the picture of the distribution of the data, observe the outliers, and demonstrate initial associations.

4. **Correlation Analysis**

   Many metrics are intercorrelated (e.g., lines of code [LOC] and WMC), so correlation analysis is conducted to identify redundant metrics. This identifies the need for factor analysis to address multicollinearity.

5. **Factor Analysis**

   The metrics are aggregated into latent factors that represent the broad categories of software characteristics (e.g., complexity, inheritance depth, coupling intensity, etc.).

6. **Determine Number of Factors**

   Techniques such as Eigenvalue analysis or the Scree plot are used to determine how many factors adequately represent the dataset.

7. **Factor Rotation**

   Rotational methods (e.g., Varimax) simplify interpretation by clarifying which metrics load heavily onto each factor.

8. **Interpret Factors**

   Each factor is interpreted in the context of software engineering. For instance, a factor loading heavily on WMC, RFC, and LOC may be labeled structural complexity.

9. **Confirmatory Factor Analysis (CFA)**

   The identified factors are validated statistically to confirm that the grouping is robust and consistent across datasets.

10. **Regression Analysis**

    The latent factors are then fed into a multiple linear regression model to predict fault-proneness. This improves stability and predictive accuracy compared to raw metrics.

11. **Model Evaluation**

    The statistical measures to assess the quality of the regression model include R^2, Adjusted R^2, F statistics, and P values.

12. **Results Interpretation**

    Lastly, regression model outputs are understood to make practically relevant decisions in a DevSecOps pipeline (such as by indicating modules with high predicted fault risk as testing and code review candidates).

2.2.1 Mathematical Form (FA and Regression)

$$Y=\beta 0+\beta 1F1+\beta 2F2+\ldots+\beta mFm+\varepsilon Y$$

Where:

- F1,F2,...,Fm: Latent factors from FA
- βi: Regression weights
- Y: Fault-proneness score or number of defects

This approach capitalizes on the two worlds:

- Factor analysis for dimensionality reduction and de-correlation
- Regression for prediction and quantitative modeling

2.3 Model Evaluation and Goodness of Fit

A fault-prediction model is not the whole equation. The second and more significant part is assessing the extent to which the model predicts clinical faults. A model might be nice on paper, but once it fails to forecast failures in practice, it is of little use. Thus, different statistical scores are used to determine the level of goodness of fit (i.e., the level to which the predicted values of the model are related to actual values).

The most widely employed metrics of evaluation are as follows:

- **R-squared (R^2):** The ratio of the variance in the dependent variable (e.g., the number of faults) to the independent variables (metrics or factors). The value of R^2 is higher, which means that the model explains the variability of the data better.
- **Adjusted R^2**: An improvement of R^2 that includes the predictors in the model. Adjusted R^2 avoids this scenario by punishing unneeded predictors, unlike the raw R^2, which always increases as a result of adding more variables to the model Adjusted R^2 helps prevent overfitting.
- **Standard Fault of Estimate (SEE):** The mean difference between values obtained and values projected. The smaller the SEE value, the more accurate the prediction.
- **F-statistic:** Tests the significance of the regression model in general. It establishes whether a predictor variable is statistically significant in terms of explaining variance on the dependent variable.
- **P-values:** Indicate the likelihood of a relationship between the predictor and the dependent variable (i.e., fault prediction) accompanied by each predictor variable. Very small p-values (typically less than 0.05) indicate that there is overwhelming evidence that the predictor variable is connected to the dependent variable (i.e., fault prediction).

2.3.1 Formula for R-squared

The R^2 is computed as follows:

$$R^2 = 1 - \frac{SS_{\text{res}}}{SS_{\text{tot}}}$$

Where:

SS_{res} = Sum of squares of residuals (variation not explained by the model)

SS_{tot} = Total sum of squares (overall variation in the data)

In simple terms, R^2 is the percentage of the overall variability of the total number of software faults that the model has explained. For instance, an R^2 value of 0.75 implies that 75 percent of the variance in faults is explained by the chosen metrics, and the remaining 25 percent is explained by random chance or other elements that are not explained by the model.

2.4 Applied Case: Fault Prediction Using CK and OO Metrics

In the empirical study from the thesis, data was collected from the Tera-PROMISE repository involving five open-source software systems. The following process was followed:

1. **Metrics Used**
   a. CK metrics: WMC, DIT, NOC, CBO, RFC, LCOM
   b. OO metrics: Additional class- and method-level attributes
2. **Modeling Steps**
   a. Computed correlation matrix among metrics
   b. Extracted factors via factor analysis
   c. Used resulting factors in MLR
   d. Compared performance to standard MLR (without factor analysis)

3. **Findings**

    a. Factor analysis reduced multicollinearity

    b. Regression using latent factors had higher R^2 and lower prediction error

    c. Only a small subset of factors explained the majority of fault variance

2.4.1 Interpretation

Modules with high values on latent factors like "complexity" or "low cohesion" showed significantly higher defect counts. This supports the hypothesis that structural characteristics of software directly influence its reliability.

2.4.2 Mapping Object-Oriented Metrics to Fault-Proneness

Object-oriented (OO) metrics like those from the Chidamber and Kemerer (CK) suite are widely used in fault prediction. When processed through FA (factor analysis) and regression, they reveal interesting patterns:

- WMC (weighted methods per class) and LOC: Strong indicators of complexity
- CBO (coupling between objects) and RFC (response for a class): Indicators of coupling and interaction
- DIT (depth of inheritance tree) and NOC (number of children): Indicators of inheritance depth

These mappings allow developers to go beyond surface-level metrics and understand the structural dimensions that truly influence fault-proneness.

2.4.3 Case Example: Using the Tera-PROMISE Dataset

The study methodology was the empirical one that was used on real-world datasets in the Tera-PROMISE repository. The repository has the fault and metric data of a number of open-source software systems. The process (illustrated in Figure 2-1) consisted of:

- Obtaining CK and OO metrics
- Conducting exploratory and correlation analysis
- Applying factor analysis to extract latent predictors
- Running regression on these predictors to model fault-proneness
- Assessing the model's performance using R^2, Adjusted R^2, SEE, and F-statistics

Findings

- A few latent factors explained most of the variance in fault counts.
- Predictions using FA and regression performed better than the base regression models.
- The *Pareto principle* held: A minority of modules were responsible for the majority of faults.

This case study highlights the strength of combining statistical techniques with real-world software data to generate actionable insights.

2.4.4 Real-World Implications

- **NASA missions:** A single undetected fault (like the Mars Climate Orbiter's metric mismatch) can cost hundreds of millions. FA and regression could have flagged fault-prone modules handling unit conversions.
- **Fintech systems:** Predictive systems have the potential to outline risky modules in payment gateways, which minimizes downtime in services where seconds of downtime lead to revenue loss.
- **Microservices:** Microservices ranking in the cloud-native world is automatable, predicting which microservice is more prone to fault. DevSecOps teams can then choose which service to test or roll out.

2.5 Limitations of Purely Statistical Models in Modern Pipelines

Although regression and factor analysis go a long way toward understanding software behavior, they still have their constraints, especially in the framework of DevSecOps and microservices:

- **Static assumptions:** Regression methods are usually based on the assumption that the relationships between predictor variables (metrics) and outcome variables (faults) are linear and remain consistent. As an example, a regression model might assume that doubling the methods in a class would double the chances of faults in that class. In the real world, software systems are not likely to be subject to predictable patterns. Moreover, the fast changing nature of microservices in the DevSecOps setting leads to nonlinear behavior. Minor changes in one service can cause a ripple effect in the entire system, whereas major changes in another service can have insignificant effects. Furthermore, the statistical associations established between predictor and outcome variables at one point in time may not persist over time, due to the constant deployment cycles of microservices.
- **Granularity challenges:** Historical fault-prediction research focused primarily on class-level or module-level metrics in monolithic systems. However, microservices present a finer granularity of units, including APIs, endpoints, and/or containerized functions. Although the code size of each microservice is likely to be smaller than a monolith, each microservice may have numerous connections to other microservices. As a consequence, purely statistical models often fail to adequately capture the granularity of interactions between microservices, since metrics such as LOC or WMC lose relevance for assessing the fault-proneness of small, distributed services. Rather, the key issues in such scenarios include the communication patterns between microservices, API call dependencies, and runtime load characteristics—all of which cannot be captured through the use of traditional metrics.

- **Dynamic environments:** In DevSecOps pipelines, there is a continuous integration, testing, and deployment of software. This creates an environment where the information on the distribution is constantly changing—the same module might not work the same as it did yesterday because there are new dependencies, scaling configurations, or workloads. This means that regression models trained in a static manner using past data become obsolete and provide ineffective predictions. In their place, dynamic models are necessary—ones that update over time as new data appears or ways of learning online that can retrain without disrupting the pipeline. The level of volatility was developed using traditional regression models, which are one-time and static.
- **Overlooked security dimensions:** Classical statistical fault prediction algorithms use structural metrics of code like complexity, size, or coupling as a key source. Although helpful, they entirely disregard another vital aspect of contemporary DevSecOps security vulnerabilities. Most faults present today are not merely a result of bad design, but of insecure configurations, third-party libraries that have fallen behind the times, or behavior of runtime systems when they are under attack. As an example, a microservice of low complexity could be highly vulnerable, provided that it relies on an unpatched library. Regression and factor analysis normally do not consider these dimensions. Therefore, they can only give a partial picture of software risk. Thus, predictive approaches should include security measures (dependency scans, vulnerability reports) along with the traditional software attributes to be effective in the modern pipelines.

Machine learning, deep learning, and mixed strategies have become available due to these restrictions. These models are more flexible when it comes to detecting complex patterns and reacting to changing codebases.

2.6 Conclusion

The statistical basis of software fault prediction was discussed in this chapter. It began by explaining regression models and demonstrated the relationship between such measures as lines of code (LOC), weighted methods per class (WMC), coupling between objects (CBO), and the probability of faults. The chapter moved on to factor analysis and demonstrated that it can be applied in order to isolate latent predictors, decrease redundancy among measures, and enhance interpretability of the model. Based on the Tera-PROMISE dataset, we were able to show how these techniques can be used to get actionable information about fault-proneness in software.

Linear regression, multiple regression, and factor analysis are all components of the mathematical model of fault prediction in the modern world. They help us uncover concealed trends in software measures, quantify risk, and predict upstream defects. We also, however, admitted that pure statistical models have certain limitations. In the DevSecOps and microservices-driven world, where the code changes fast and services are connected in nonlinear and complicated ways, the statistic model regression can fall behind. These limitations underscore the necessity to have more dynamic and smart solutions. We will continue this base in the next chapter, where we discuss predictive modeling of microservice-based architectures, and how the more modern machine learning methods go beyond classical statistics. These methods allow teams to:

- Quantify risk across software components with greater accuracy
- Reduce redundancy in predictive models by learning richer feature representations
- Integrate prediction seamlessly into DevSecOps pipelines, ensuring continuous, proactive quality assurance

By blending these methods, engineers move from being reactive bug-fixers to proactive risk managers. This shift not only improves software quality but also ensures resilience in systems where failure is not an option.

The next chapter moves beyond foundations into practical modeling: building, validating, and deploying prediction models in microservice-based DevSecOps environments.

PART II

Embedding Prediction into CI/CD Pipelines

CHAPTER 3

Integrating Fault Prediction into CI/CD Pipelines

Modern software delivery pipes are engineered to be fast, and being fast does not make the process stable. In fact, it can result in failures that propagate across production. Building fault prediction into CI/CD pipelines offers an early-warning system, one that can identify defects before they become apparent in the production process. Chapter 2 discussed constructing and validating predictive models. It is only when those models are placed into the delivery workflows that they are valuable, because they give real-time information and affect release choices. Chapter 2 showed how to make such integrations work. It discussed automated fault-detection mechanisms, supporting tools and feedback loops that ensure that models perform well over time.

This chapter is about implementing those models. It examines the design of automated fault-detection mechanisms, tools, and frameworks that can facilitate integrating and monitoring feedback loops that allow the system to continue to improve over time.

3.1 Designing Automated Fault-Detection Mechanisms

The previous chapter discussed how prediction models can be constructed, assessed, and verified using past data. However, a model in a lab notebook or a Jupyter environment is not itself valuable. The actual transformation occurs once such models are incorporated into the software delivery pipeline, where they can actively stop fault-prone code from being delivered to production.

D. Sharma and A. Syed, *Fault Detection in Microservice Architectures*,
https://doi.org/10.1007/979-8-8688-2712-9_3

This chapter is concerned with this change: transforming research-quality models into practical CI/CD checks. It is aimed at translating prediction theory into practice, so that each pull request, build, or deployment is enhanced with automated foresight. Fault prediction in CI/CD pipelines can be achieved by initially adding automated checks at key stages in the pipeline. The pipeline itself is a gatekeeper that inspects code, dependencies, configurations, and even templates of infrastructure-as-code (IaC). The goal is to detect risks at an earlier stage rather than waiting until after deployment monitoring to detect the problem.

Key design considerations include:

1. **Shift-left analysis**

   Fault prediction is most valuable when implemented at the earliest opportunity. Predictive checks during the pull request phase will guarantee that potentially fault-prone code is not introduced into the main branch. This is in line with the DevSecOps philosophy of shifting left, where testing and risk analysis occur as close to the point of code creation as possible, as opposed to occurring after publication. The early integration of predictions provides developers with immediate feedback, resulting in them being able to make corrections sooner, when the code is fresh in their memory. This lowers rework and the chances of a fault occurring downstream. The sooner a fault is identified, the cheaper and easier it is to rectify. That is why predictive models should be run as close to the point of code creation as possible. By integrating predictive checks into pull requests, developers get insight into real-time feedback prior to their code being incorporated into the main branch.

   Suppose a developer has made a PR with changes that are made on a historically fault-prone module. The model uses complexity, churn, and dependency measures, after which it gives a high-risk score. The system may propose additional peer review, perform further tests, or ask for a senior engineer endorsement instead of simply combining with the other peer review. Not only is this fault prediction serving as an intelligent assistant, but it is also shifting potential fault to the left, directly instilling quality thought into the developer process.

2. **Multi-stage integration**

   Although early checks are very important, one stage is not enough. Code is dynamic it undergoes changes as it passes through the pipeline; various risks are involved at various times. Automated fault detection should be a layered defense that builds, tests, and deploys checkpoints to be effective. Fault prediction must be intertwined with the pipeline at various points:

   - **Build stage:** Predictive models evaluate metrics such as code complexity, churn, and dependency vulnerabilities, flagging modules that are statistically likely to fail. Predictive models analyze structural metrics (complexity, duplication, and dependency risks) and flag components that are statistically likely to fail.
   - **Testing stage:** Anomaly-detection systems analyze unit, integration, and regression test results to spot unusual behavior patterns that might indicate hidden faults.
   - **Deployment stage:** Risk scores are applied to build artifacts, indicating whether they should move forward to staging or production. Although a build artifact might have a high-risk score, it may be permissible to deploy the artifact to a staging environment with additional monitoring.

   Such a stratified solution is similar to the principle of the safety nets—if one barrier fails to indicate a problem, the next control point heightens the chances of it being identified. This approach allows one gate to fail on a problem, because another has an opportunity to intercept it. Again, as in aviation or safety-critical engineering, checks are redundant, which enhances resilience.

3. **Contextual risk scoring**

   Not all of the prediction flags are supposed to close the pipeline completely. The binary pass/fail system may be frustrating to developers and will lower adoption. Rather, it is more successful when fault prediction is used to implement risk-based controls.

One example is a module that has a moderate likelihood of failure. This can cause more automated tests to be run and perhaps require a peer review before being merged. This subtle methodology is a balance between speed and safety. The predictions made are based on decision-making and do not halt the progress unnecessarily. Risk-based actions should be run on predictions rather than hard pass/fail gates. In contrast, fault prediction is more effective when risk-based and proportional controls are used.

For example:

- A module with a moderate fault probability may trigger additional automated tests but not block the build.
- A high-risk score might enforce a mandatory peer review or staged rollout.
- Only critical risks should result in a hard failure that halts the pipeline.

Organizations balance speed and safety by scaling responses to risk. Forecasting does not halt an action that does not warrant it. This is a subtle compromise that strikes a balance between speed and safety without losing developer trust.

Automation with guardrails

Trust is the key to success of any predictive system. Developers should feel that the system is assisting them, not punishing them. That credibility is due to transparency and usability. Explicit reasons as to why a module was flagged and the next steps to follow take fault prediction from a black-box system to a usable guide. If the service is blocked, the report must contain a statement that the complexity score is too big, coverage is minimal, and overall historical bug density is high.

Exception handling is also imperative. Sometimes, teams might skip a prediction so that they can make an urgent fix or experiment. Allowing countermeasures will avoid frustration while maintaining general responsibility. Predictive checks serve as guardrails to help teams make safer decisions; they do not serve as strict barriers. Developers understand that fault prediction is not about bureaucracy, but it is a safety net that they trust so they can move at a faster pace.

Fault prediction is not a one-time check but an ongoing process that learns using historical defect data and evolves as the codebase changes. Fault prediction must not be seen as punitive by the developers. That means:

- Clear reporting on *why* a module was flagged
- Exception handling for edge cases
- Actionable remediation steps

When integrated this way, predictions become confidence-building guardrails, not frustrating blockers. Developing automated fault-detection mechanisms is a matter of combining the future-oriented perspective and the practicality. Issues are identified during shift-left integration. Multi-stage checkpoints are resilient. Necessary friction is avoided in risk-based controls. Guardrails guarantee adoption by ensuring that the experience of developing it remains positive. See Figure 3-1 describes automated fault detection across CI/CD stages. The next step is to explore the tools and frameworks that make this integration possible, thereby turning design into reality.

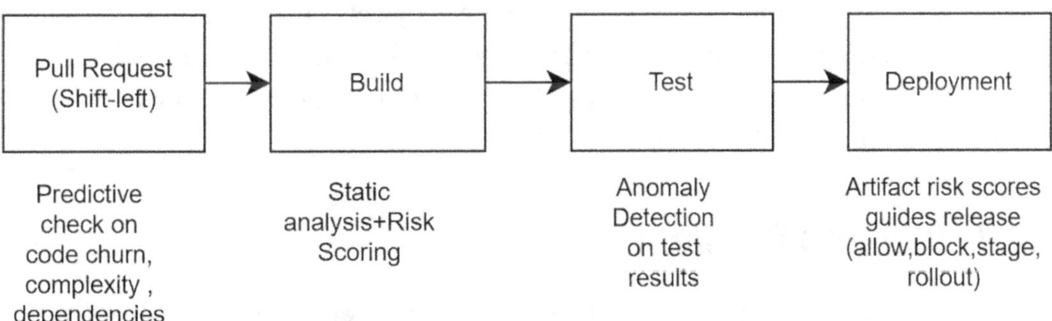

Figure 3-1. *Automated fault detection across CI/CD stages*

3.2 Tools and Frameworks for Integration

Once fault-prediction mechanisms are designed, the next step is to bring them to life inside a CI/CD pipeline. Fortunately, most modern pipelines—whether Jenkins, GitHub Actions, GitLab CI, or Azure DevOps—are highly extensible. This allows teams to plug in both ready-made tools and custom models to support predictive fault detection.

3.2.1 Static and Predictive Analysis Tools

Static analysis tools provide the foundation for fault prediction by continuously evaluating code quality and complexity. They also generate the historical metrics needed to train predictive models:

- **SonarQube/CodeQL:** These platforms analyze source code against customizable rulesets, flagging security vulnerabilities, code smells, and bug-prone patterns. Over time, the metrics collected (e.g., cyclomatic complexity, duplicated lines, dependency issues) feed directly into fault-prediction models.
- **PMD and Checkstyle:** These lightweight tools can be augmented with custom rules that evaluate predictive risk factors. They integrate seamlessly into most CI/CD platforms and can halt builds based on configurable thresholds.
- **Custom static analyzers:** For organizations that want more tailored predictions, models built using scikit-learn, TensorFlow, or R packages can be embedded as pipeline jobs. These models can incorporate organization-specific signals, such as code churn or past defect history, to produce risk scores more aligned with the team's environment. For organizations with specific needs, custom analyzers can be built using frameworks like ANTLR or AST parsers. These tools can implement proprietary fault-prediction algorithms tailored to specific codebases or domains.

3.2.2 Test and Quality Gates

Predictive analytics is strengthened when paired with rigorous testing and coverage tools. These tools help correlate fault-prone areas with gaps in testing.

- **JaCoCo:** Tracks unit test and integration test coverage, highlighting weakly tested modules that are already marked as high-risk by prediction models.

- **Mutation testing frameworks (PIT for Java, MutPy for Python):** Go beyond coverage by deliberately introducing small faults ("mutations") to the code and checking if the test suite catches them. A weak test suite that misses these faults indicates that real defects may slip through undetected.

3.2.3 CI/CD-Native Integrations

Predictive fault detection can be integrated into the current CI/CD programs with ease; this is one of the main benefits of this approach. Instead of necessitating a completely new infrastructure, fault-prediction mechanisms can be directly implemented on the development platforms that are already familiar. This enables predictive checks to run in parallel with current build, test, and deployment processes, all with minimal disturbance to established practices.

The following sections discuss the CI/CD platforms and machine learning (ML) systems that are often used as integration points. This section is especially directed at students, as well as those who are new to these tools.

CI/CD Platforms

Modern CI/CD platforms provide multiple integration points for fault prediction:

- **Jenkins plugins:** Jenkins is one of the original and most used CI/CD automation servers. It provides a wide range of plugins, which integrate with static analysis tools, testing systems, and predictive models. Jenkins pipelines can call ML predictors with Groovy-based scripting, and risk scores can be presented simultaneously with traditional quality checks. The Pipeline Stage View also allows greater transparency by visualizing the results of risk assessment using various stages. Most of the static analysis tools have Pipeline Stage View plugins. Proprietary fault-prediction models can be integrated with custom plugins Jenkins and can call ML-based predictors as part of the build and test processes to ensure that predictions run like other CI/CD workflows.
- **GitHub Actions:** GitHub Actions is a closely integrated automation platform in the GitHub universe. Code pushes, pull requests, or scheduled events may trigger workflows. GitHub Actions is based

on predictive fault detection and presents results in pull request discussions. It is possible to use custom GitHub Actions or the GitHub Check Runs API to include interactive reports with reasons why specific files or modules were identified as high-risk. Workflows can be set to run predictive jobs on each push or pull request. An example might be a module that is fault-prone automatically perform extra security scans or regression checks. Specific actions can be developed to execute fault-prediction models as part of a pull request. GitHub Check Runs API enables teams to build rich interactive reports that reveal why certain files or changes are considered high-risk.

- **GitLab CI/CD**: Gitlab is a platform that combines version control and CI/CD, with easy feedback loops between development and deployment. Custom runners and pipeline jobs can be used to run predictive analytics. Findings can be surfaced directly to merge request interfaces via GitLab widgets. This enables reviewers to evaluate not only functional correctness but also the risk of predicted faults before merging changes. fault-prediction also supports arbitrary runners to run predictive analytics scripts, and thus both open-source ML and custom models can be used. GitLab's merge request widgets are capable of showing results of fault prediction directly in the merge request interface. Custom pipeline jobs can also compute risk scores and transfer them between stages with the help of artifacts.

- **Azure DevOps**: Azure DevOps is a popular enterprise project that integrates release management, pipelines, and repositories. Custom pipeline tasks can be used to include fault prediction, but the Azure DevOps REST API can be used to develop dashboards that track the performance of predictive models. This enables tracking the accuracy, recall, and general predictive reliability in the long run, which is crucial in organizations that have lengthy release periods. Custom tasks can be used to predict faults during the construction and release of pipelines. Azure DevOps REST API allows the teams to develop dashboards that monitor the accuracy of fault prediction and the performance of the system over the time.

ML Infrastructure for Prediction

Whereas initial fault-prediction solutions may be based on direct scripting or lightweight APIs, advanced implementations use a dedicated ML infrastructure. These are used to track experiments and deploy at scale as fault-prediction models continue to become more sophisticated:

- **MLflow:** MLflow is an open-source machine learning lifecycle management platform. It offers model versioning, reproducibility, and tracking of experiments. In the framework of CI/CD, MLflow allows an organization to deploy modified prediction models in a gradual way and maintain past versions to roll back or use for comparative analysis. MLflow offers model versioning, experiment tracking, and deployment. It also allows teams to handle many versions of fault-prediction models and roll out improvements.
- **Azure ML and AWS SageMaker:** Azure machine learning, as well as Amazon SageMaker, offer trained, deployed, and monitored ML models on managed clouds. They are especially suitable in a large-scale setting where predictive models need to be made available as scalable endpoints. Their A/B testing and automatic scaling characteristics are useful in fault-prediction conditions that have a changing predictive accuracy over time, and they provide endpoints into which fault-prediction models can be served. These platforms do scaling, versioning, and A/B testing of various models.
- **Kubeflow:** Kubeflow is an ML platform used in Kubernetes setups. It offers the entire process of creating, training, and deploying ML models as microservices. Models of fault prediction deployed on Kubeflow can be accessed using HTTP APIs and are therefore simple to integrate into CI/CD pipelines. For organizations that already have invested in the Kubernetes, Kubeflow is a natural extension of the infrastructure they already have. Kubeflow is a full ML workflow platform to teams that use Kubernetes. Fault-prediction models can also be implemented in the form of microservices, which can be connected to CI/CD pipelines via HTTP APIs.

- **Custom ML APIs:** Full-scale ML infrastructure is not always needed, and in these situations, prediction models may be served as lightweight APIs with FastAPI or Flask. These APIs provide fault-prediction services as REST endpoints, which may be invoked directly in CI/CD scripts. It is a very flexible method that may be quickly prototyped and deployed alongside the existing build infrastructure. Fault-prediction models may be served through simple REST APIs written in languages such as FastAPI or Flask. These lightweight services can be implemented with a CI/CD infrastructure and invoked by pipeline scripts.

For practitioners, the key insight is that predictive fault detection does not exist in isolation. Its effectiveness depends on seamless integration into the CI/CD systems that already govern software delivery. Entry-level implementations may begin with simple scripting within Jenkins or GitHub Actions. As models mature, organizations can adopt ML lifecycle management tools such as MLflow or cloud-based solutions like SageMaker. Ultimately, the integration strategy should balance predictive sophistication with operational simplicity, ensuring that predictions augment rather than obstruct development workflows (see Table 3-1).

Table 3-1. *CI/CD platforms and ML Infrastructure for Fault Prediction*

Category	Tool/ Platform	Key Features	Strengths Related to Fault Prediction	Best Suited For
CI/CD platform	Jenkins	Plugin ecosystem, Groovy scripting, Pipeline Stage View	Mature ecosystem; can run ML predictors in build/test stages; risk scores shown in pipeline stages	Organizations with legacy CI/CD setups; teams requiring maximum customization
	GitHub Actions	Workflow automation within GitHub, Check Runs API, PR integration	Predictions shown directly in pull request; custom actions for ML integration	Open-source projects; teams using GitHub as primary repo

(*continued*)

Table 3-1. *(continued)*

Category	Tool/ Platform	Key Features	Strengths Related to Fault Prediction	Best Suited For
	Gitlab CI/CD	Built-in CI/CD with version control, custom runners, MR widgets	Fault risk reports embedded in merge requests; simple artifact handling	Enterprises needing all-in-one DevOps and CI/CD integration
	Azure DevOps	Pipelines, REST API, dashboards	Predictive results tracked over time; integrates with enterprise systems	Large organizations, especially Microsoft ecosystem adopters
ML lifecycle/ infrastructure	MLflow	Model versioning, experiment tracking, deployment	Enables incremental rollout of updated models; ensures reproducibility	Teams experimenting with evolving fault predictors
	Azure ML	Cloud-managed ML, scalable endpoints, A/B testing	Managed infra reduces overhead; suited for enterprise pipelines	Organizations already invested in Azure
	AWS SageMaker	Managed ML lifecycle, deployment endpoints, monitoring	Strong scaling support; rich integration with AWS CI/CD	Teams using AWS-native CI/CD or hybrid ML workflows
	Kubeflow	Kubernetes-native ML platform, microservices deployment	Models as microservices; integrates seamlessly with K8s CI/CD	Cloud-native orgs running containerized microservices
	Custom ML APIs (FastAPI/ Flask)	Lightweight REST endpoints for models	Quick prototyping; low overhead; flexible deployment	Small teams, research groups, or early-stage pilots

3.2.4 Data and Logging Infrastructure

The strength of prediction models is limited only by the strength of the data. Even the best model will give unreliable results if the underlying data is incomplete, noisy, or managed poorly. With fault prediction in CI/CD pipelines, it would mean that every run of a build, test, or deployment would capture detailed metrics, which are then stored and analyzed in order to reduce model accuracy continuously. The developers and stakeholders must also be in a position to view the results. Visualizations create trust by making the system transparent and actionable.

Elasticsearch/Kibana

Elasticsearch provides a scalable and efficient way to store large volumes of pipeline logs and metrics. Every time a build runs, the system can log details such as:

- Commit metadata (who made the change, which files were modified)
- Code complexity and static analysis results
- Test outcomes and coverage statistics
- Fault-prediction scores generated by ML models

After indexing this information in Elasticsearch, Kibana becomes the visualization layer. Using Kibana dashboards, teams can see patterns rapidly. For example, they can see which components are always thought to be fault-prone or performance trends in prediction accuracy between projects. These insights also assist teams in improving their models over time, as they can determine the points of prediction congruency or deviations in their predictions against the real reports of defects.

As a practical example, suppose we have a dashboard that indicates the top five most prone-to-failure modules this quarter and shows the evidence behind this (both the predictions and the actual bugs). This visibility type gives engineering leads the ability to give priority reviews, assign testing resources, and monitor the long-term improvement of the model.

Prometheus/Grafana

Prometheus and Grafana are effective in real-time monitoring where Elasticsearch and Kibana are superior in the storage and analysis of logs. Prometheus collects metrics on the CI/CD systems and prediction services on a regularly scheduled basis and Grafana displays them in dynamic dashboards and alerts.

For fault prediction, some key metrics to monitor might include:

- **Pipeline health:** Build durations, failure rates, and test pass/fail ratios.
- **Model performance:** Precision, recall, and F1-scores of predictions compared to actual defect outcomes.
- **Drift indicators:** Signs that the model's accuracy is degrading, such as an increase in false positives or false negatives.

As an example, a Grafana dashboard can display a real-time chart of Prediction Accuracy Over Last 30 Days, and teams can note when retraining is necessary. Alerts can be set in such a way that when the precision becomes less than 70 percent, the team is automatically alerted to investigate.

In the absence of effective data and monitoring infrastructure, fault-prediction models will be dismissed or discredited. The developers will be more willing to trust predictive outcomes when they observe evidence in clear dashboards, with past trends and real-time error rates. With Elasticsearch/Kibana used as a solution to analyze past trends and Prometheus/Grafana as a solution to monitor the current situation, organizations establish an environment that is highly feedback-driven. Fault prediction is not an abstract concept in theory but a stable and constantly evolving component of the CI/CD pipeline. When combined, Prometheus and Grafana can turn a black-box system into a measurable, auditable, and trustworthy fault-prediction system.

3.3 Implementation Patterns

3.3.1 Pipeline-as-Code Integration

Modern CI/CD pipelines are increasingly defined as code, making it easier to version and manage fault-prediction integration:

Example GitHub Actions workflow with fault prediction

```
name: CI/CD with Fault Prediction
on: [push, pull_request]
jobs:
  fault-prediction:
    runs-on: ubuntu-latest
    steps:
      - uses: actions/checkout@v2
      - name: Run Fault Prediction
        id: predict
        run: |
          # Extract code metrics
          python scripts/extract_metrics.py --output metrics.json
          # Run prediction model
          risk_score=$(python scripts/predict_faults.py --metrics
          metrics.json)
          echo "::set-output name=risk_score::$risk_score"

      - name: Gate Deployment
        if: steps.predict.outputs.risk_score > 0.8
        run: |
          echo "High risk detected. Requiring additional approvals."
          exit 1
```

3.3.2 Pipeline-as-Code Example (GitHub Actions)

```
name: CI/CD with Fault Prediction
on: [push, pull_request]

jobs:
  fault-prediction:
    runs-on: ubuntu-latest
    steps:
      - uses: actions/checkout@v2
      - name: Run Fault Prediction
        run: |
```

```
    python scripts/extract_metrics.py --output metrics.json
    risk_score=$(python scripts/predict_faults.py --metrics
    metrics.json)
    if (( $(echo "$risk_score > 0.8" | bc -l) )); then exit 1; fi
```

3.3.3 Microservices Architecture

For large organizations, fault prediction can be implemented as a set of microservices:

Example FastAPI service for fault prediction

```
from fastapi import FastAPI
from pydantic import BaseModel
import joblib

app = FastAPI()
model = joblib.load('fault_prediction_model.pkl')

class CodeMetrics(BaseModel):
    complexity: float
    churn_rate: float
    test_coverage: float
    dependencies: int
@app.post("/predict")
async def predict_fault_risk(metrics: CodeMetrics):
    features = [metrics.complexity, metrics.churn_rate,
                metrics.test_coverage, metrics.dependencies]
    risk_score = model.predict_proba([features])[0][1]
    return {
        "risk_score": risk_score,
        "recommendation": "require_review" if risk_score > 0.7 else
        "proceed"
    }
```

3.3.4 Putting It All Together

The best system is a combination of off-the-shelf tools that offer instant quality monitoring with tailor-made predictive models that have been trained using the defect history of the organization. This hybrid model ensures that overall best practices and domain-specific insights are both implemented. The outcome is a pipeline that not only pushes software but also takes positive action to minimize the risk of failure with each commit.

3.4 Conclusion

Fault prediction should not be considered a replacement of traditional testing practices but rather an enhancement of them with foresight. The predictive models covered in Chapter 2 can only be valued in the real sense when they are directly incorporated into the delivery process and used to identify risks. The right combination of tools and frameworks supported by automated detection mechanisms results in an early-warning system that ensures that high-risk changes do not quietly creep to production.

Monitoring and feedback loops are also significant. These guarantee that all the errors found during testing or after the release to the system are fed back into the system, making the system accurate and relevant. The outcome is a self-enhancing safety net that not only minimizes rework and operational firefighting but also establishes trust and reliability with every release.

The implementation of fault prediction into the pipeline itself will transform the CI/CD system into a smart, quality watchdog that will constantly learn, evolve, and protect the integrity of the software.

CHAPTER 4

Monitoring and Feedback Loops: Why Prediction Models Need Constant Recalibration

4.1 Introduction

Predictive fault detection using software systems is not a one-time effort. There are also bound to be changes in the behavior of models due to the dynamics of the underlying data, codebase, and development practices. This is usually referred to as *concept drift* and it takes place when the statistical properties of the input variables change over time.

For example, a model that has been trained on fault patterns in a monolithic architecture may not be effective after an organization has embraced microservices. Predictive models require a monitoring and feedback loop environment in order to be accurate. These loops enable the models to be continuously tested and updated with new information. Without such recalibration, accuracy suffers, and this leads to false guarantees and defects. A good fault-prediction system is determined by feedback. Current predictions will not pass the test of time unless they are recalibrated with new data. To ensure that these models are always accurate and helpful, they must be checked constantly.

D. Sharma and A. Syed, *Fault Detection in Microservice Architectures*,
https://doi.org/10.1007/979-8-8688-2712-9_4

4.2 Core Elements of Effective Feedback Loops

The system of fault prediction is based on feedback loops. Without them, predictions soon become outdated, false, and pointless. A feedback loop ensures that the system is always learning and changing. The core elements of effective feedback loops are discussed in the following sections.

4.2.1 Prediction Accuracy Tracking

One should test the level of correspondence between the predictions of the model and the reality. This includes comparisons between the modules identified as fault-prone and the actual defects found during testing or production. The patterns of false positives (modules flagged without faults), and false negatives (faults were predicted but did not happen) can be determined with the help of this comparison. Dashboards should track such measures as precision, recall, and F1 Score over time.

As an example, a Grafana dashboard could visualize the number of high-risk modules that the model estimated last month and developers could instantly receive feedback on whether the model is working. With such measures being monitored on a regular basis, stakeholders can have confidence and take action. The first component of a feedback loop is a rigid evaluation of the predictive performance. The three metrics used in determining the software quality of machine learning are precision, recall, and F1 Score.

- **Precision:** The number of predicted fault-prone modules.
- **Recall:** The percentage of actual faulty modules that the model identifies.
- **F1 Score:** The arithmetic mean of the precision and the recall, which is a weighted average of the two. Precision and recall are the combination of the two.

These metrics should not only be monitored during model deployment but also during the lifecycle of the software. For example, as a dependency is added, accuracy may decrease, but recall may also increase as a bug database is added. A pulse check of the model's health would be a continuous dashboard of these metrics.

4.2.2 Data Enrichment

The predictive model, like its data training data, is good. As soon as the bugs are removed and logs of incidents and user commentary are fed back into the system, this will augment the dataset, but predictive power can hardly be sustained on static code metrics alone. The research on fault prediction has determined that fault occurrence is no longer predicted by the static code metrics in the presence of a microservice environment (Qiu et al., 2024). Continuous data enhancement adds dynamic signals like error metrics (Phung et al., 2025) and churn indicators based on the domain.

A robust feedback loop must continuously enrich the training data with evolving features:

- **Bugs:** New defects are registered as new label occurrences. Severity, resolution time, and parts utilized all increase model context.
- **Churn:** Code churn measures how frequently files are modified, which often signals instability. A file rewritten five times in one release cycle deserves more weight in prediction.
- **Dependencies:** External system vulnerabilities, API changes, or even changes to the build system should lead to a changing risk profile. The dependency metadata will be recorded and reentered.

The model is comparable to the dynamic nature of software projects, as it will tie these signals into retraining pipelines. When such data points are included with more context sensitive features, the model can be more sensitive to the specifics of the risk trends that can otherwise be characterized by code metrics.

4.2.3 Adaptive Thresholds for Different Domains

Not every area is equal. A safety-critical automotive ECU requires false negatives (high recall), but false positives (high precision) can be significant to an e-commerce frontend. Adaptive thresholds, which indicate domain-based risk appetites, should be enabled by the use of feedback loops. For instance:

- In medical programs, recall can cause serious life errors. The boundaries have to be biased toward recall to the disadvantage of accuracy.

- False alarm flagging in consumer apps annoys the developers and users. Accuracy becomes the prevailing measure. These are the limits that cannot be predetermined.

The cycle time of the release must be reassessed according to the real-life experiences of the output of productions. In a safety-critical system (e.g., automotive software or medical device), a low probability of failure may even lead to mandated code inspection or additional testing. On the other hand, with a non-critical web application, intervention can be required, but only be in the form of modules that have a high chance of failure. Adaptive thresholds—be it in safety, efficiency, or developer productivity—provide a trade-off.

4.2.4 Human-in-the-Loop Reviews

Automated prediction is a powerful instrument, but human judgment cannot be dismissed. Developers should have an opportunity to comment on the list of modules that have been identified as true positives and false positives and to provide background on the anomalies. It is possible to use these inputs to reassign the model in a more desirable manner. This can be seen in the situation whereby a module is always flagged, yet defects are not observed. The model can adjust the weighting or the significance of features to reduce unnecessary notifications. This type of cooperation renders the predictions viable and, consequently, not neglected due to the exhaustion of alerts. If a prediction model finds faults in a module 52 percent of the time, is this actionable? Should developers explore this? Human-in-the-loop (HITL) reviews create a brevity of context in this case. Predictions can be validated by senior engineers or QA leads who need to offer annotations and override reasons on corner cases. Such annotations cannot be remote. They need to be reintroduced into the training information. The model would correct its mistakes over time, likewise in the correction of the expert.

4.2.5 Continuous Retraining and Versioning

Fault-prediction models experience degradation over time as a result of changes in the codebase. To ensure that retraining is accurate, it should be automated on a monthly, quarterly, or event-based basis. To keep several versions of the models, a team may use model versioning software, such as MLflow or DVC, in the CI/CD pipelines. The team can then keep track of variations in model performance across time and release new versions of the model without breaking the code. This constantly feeds enhancements into the delivery procedure without introducing a pause in the development process.

A system cannot have incomplete feedback loops in the absence of systematic retraining. Two key enablers stand out:

- **MLflow:** Facilitates experiment tracking, model packaging, and deployment monitoring. Each retrained model can be versioned, compared, and rolled back if performance degrades.
- **DVC (Data Version Control):** Extends Git workflows to manage datasets, model checkpoints, and feature pipelines. This ensures reproducibility, a critical property in regulated industries.

By integrating MLflow and DVC into CI/CD pipelines, teams can establish a closed loop where models are retrained automatically as new labeled data arrives, yet all versions remain auditable.

By embedding this cycle of monitoring and feedback, organizations ensure that fault prediction becomes smarter over time, transforming CI/CD pipelines into adaptive systems that both deliver and defend.

4.3 Practical Visualization of Feedback Loops

Monitoring principles are abstract principles, which in fact are attributed to a tangible value when visualized. Grafana and Kibana provide the user with the opportunity to visualize feedback loops within the teams because of their intuitive dashboards.

Dashboard components include:

- **Model accuracy panel:** The accuracy, recall, and F1 graph in various releases in real time.
- **Integration bug feed:** Real-time updates of consumed new defects, including severity and layer.
- **Churn heatmaps:** Accessing files or files under change.
- **Triggering system:** The default triggers are usually threshold-based triggers (e.g., an alarm is triggered when the recall of a critical subsystem becomes less than 0.7). Calibration and feature drift, along with accuracy, are expected to be visualized with Kibana and Grafana panels.

Grafana and Kibana panels should visualize calibration and feature drift along with accuracy. Recommended panels include:

- **Calibration histogram (ECE plot):** Predicted probability vs. observed defect frequency.
- **Feature entropy trend:** Tracks dominant ATE-weighted metrics that change over releases.
- **Model lifecycle index:** Aggregates precision, recall, ECE, and FPSI (Qiu et al., 2024) to score overall model health.

These dashboards transform noncommunicative data into a severe notification, and this fosters transparency between the development and QA team. With the help of MLflow and DVC in CI/CD pipelines, it is possible to establish a closed loop, where retraining of models automatically happens when new labeled data is available, but where all versions are not auditable. With this monitoring and feedback loop, organizations become more intelligent with fault prediction across time. CI/CD pipelines are transformed into reactionary systems, which leads to defensive and offensive capabilities.

4.4 Case Illustration

Consider the case of a financial services company applying a financial fault-prediction model to its algorithmic trading system. This is a scenario where capital exposure is directly influenced by milliseconds and model fidelity. This was done by training the predictive engine on the churn and error-type measures (Phung et al., 2025) and object-oriented factors as identified by factor analysis.

The model offered an F1 of 0.82 and an Expected Calibration Error of 0.11, which is a terrific starting point on which to filter faults in release pipes. Three months later, the recall dropped to 0.65 when the ECE upsurged to 0.27, accompanied by a series of third-party API integration failures that had happened during the Knight Capital failure (Boe Hee Min et al., 2022). Calibration dashboards on Grafana were used to raise alerts when the ECE crossed the set limit of 10 percent. Root cause Signals Neighborhood Rough Sets analysis (Jiang et al., 2025) was used to trace root cause signals to new dependency libraries, where a change frequency had changed feature distributions and AT E causality assumptions were violated.

By marking false negatives as human-in-the-loop, engineers labeled false negatives on API-heavy modules, providing context that updated the training repository. When retraining was done with error-type augmentations and dependency metadata, it decreased ECE to 0.09 and recovered F1 to 0.84. High-risk financial modules and relaxed accuracy of non-critical dashboards increased recall requirements and minimized precision. In this case, adaptive domain thresholds were implemented.

This example shows how active monitoring and calibration-feedback-loop prevented the silent Knight-type cascade of faults, which were converted to an informative retraining loop. It demonstrates how active monitoring and calibration feedback loops prevent silent model decay.

4.5 Challenges and Pitfalls

One challenge is *feedback overload,* which is when there are too many signals on retraining pipelines. Empirical research indicates that drift monitors can generate contradictory signals in sets of features that overinflate false drift alarms (Shahini et al., 2025). There have to be priorities.

- **Data quality issues:** There might be duplications or problems with poor labels of the bug trackers or the rating of the severity might be inconsistent. Garbage in, garbage out. Apparently, duplicated and inconsistent bugs in the duplicated labels of severity hamper model precision. Neighborhood Rough-Set Checks initiated before retraining eliminate entries that noisiest (Jiang et al., 2025).
- **Human fatigue:** Human-in-the-loop reviews are sometime overused, leading to review fatigue. Automation has to take a middle ground.
- **Tooling fragmentation:** Integrating MLflow, DVC, Grafana, and bug-tracking tools requires disciplined DevOps practices.

4.6 Future Directions

New methods will enhance feedback loops:

- **Active learning:** Models only query humans on the most uncertain predictions, cutting down on annotation. This is based on the use of ATE-weighted uncertainty scores to query experts to minimize the cost of annotation and increase the quality of labels (Mangal & Rathore, 2025).
- **Self-healing pipelines:** Automated retraining when drift detection thresholds are crossed. AIOps agents automatically trigger NRSEL ensemble retraining once the ECE or F1 drops below governed thresholds (Jiang et al., 2025).
- **Explainable AI (XAI):** Build trust by providing interpretability measures to explain to developers why a file was flagged. The fact that the developers can see the causes of risk score changes with heatmaps of feature-importance on top of error-type description vectors can be helpful in building trust (Phung et al., 2025).
- **Cross-project transfer learning:** Bootstrapping one domain with feedback from another domain. Calibrated models transfer meta-weights across projects without revealing data and increase generalization in multi-tenant settings (Qiu et al., 2024).

These advancements signal a future where predictive models will not only adapt but will also justify their adaptations.

4.7 Conclusion

Monitoring and feedback loops are the scaffolding responsible for maintaining predictive fault detection in living software systems. Precision, recall, and F1 are the baseline measures, but actual value is achieved by applying defects, churn measures, and dependency insights. Adaptive thresholds, human reviews, and retraining pipelines provide resilience to drift. Lastly, feedback is made actionable with the help of visualization tools such as Grafana and Kibana. Recalibration is not a decision made in a few occasions but rather is a constant undertaking. Models are supposed to vary with software and data changes. Through these critical feedback systems, organizations can ensure that their predictive systems are reliable.

PART III

Applied Case Studies

CHAPTER 5

Case Study: Fault Prediction in an E-Commerce Microservices Pipeline

5.1 Introduction

E-commerce is now one of the most complicated digital systems in contemporary software engineering. The current enterprise-scale platforms are no longer mere web applications; they are distributed, multi-cloud event-driven, microservices-based architecture. Fault prediction has therefore become central in creating reliable, high-throughput pipelines. Modern DevOps and AI-driven observability platforms use predictive signals from logs, traces, and telemetry to detect degradation early and initiate remediation. In large production environments, predictive incident detection combined with automated remediation has been shown to reduce mean time to recovery (MTTR) by 30–45 percent, all while preventing a significant portion of customer-visible outages.

This chapter examines fault prediction in a real-world e-commerce microservice pipeline. The approach integrates traditional reliability engineering practices with AI-driven predictive models, LLM-assisted root cause analysis, and AIOps-based remediation workflows. The goal is to demonstrate how predictive intelligence can be embedded directly into modern software delivery pipelines to improve operational resilience.

D. Sharma and A. Syed, *Fault Detection in Microservice Architectures*,
https://doi.org/10.1007/979-8-8688-2712-9_5

5.2 Architectural Overview of a Modern E-Commerce Platform

A modern e-commerce platform typically spans tens to hundreds of microservices, orchestrated through Kubernetes, managed via service meshes (such as Istio or Linkerd), and observed through a unified telemetry pipeline integrating logs, traces, metrics, and events.

Figure 5-1 breaks down the architectural layers with an e-commerce application.

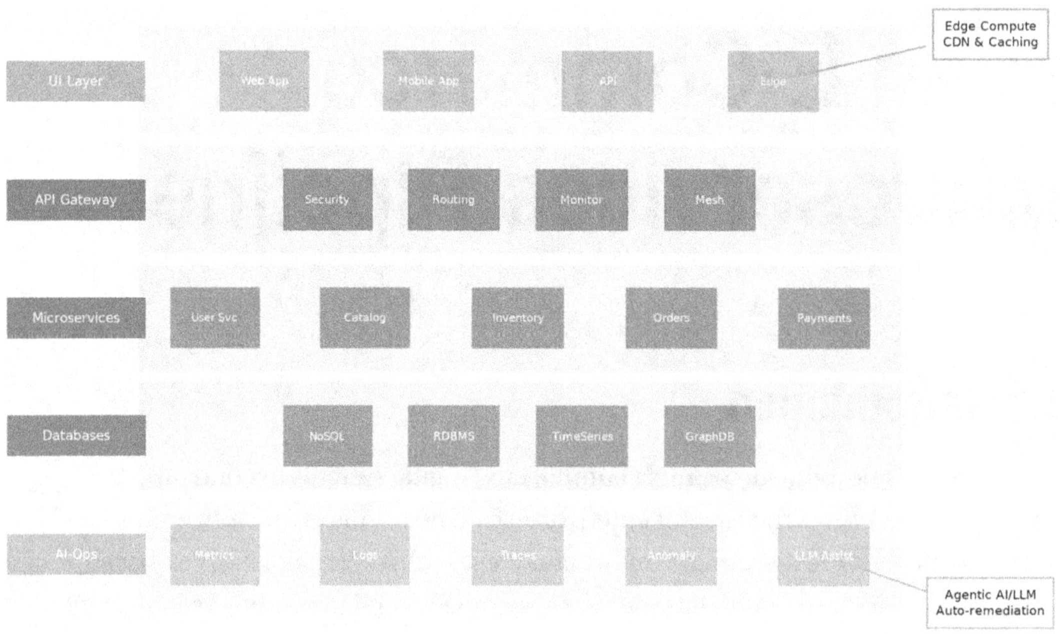

Figure 5-1. *E-commerce microservices architecture*

These layers make each other stronger. Frontends take advantage of the personalization of edge compute; gateways protect and trace downstream traffic; microservices offer isolation of business complexity; data stores optimize per-context performance; and observability augmented by agentic LLM makes production telemetry a learning constituent.

This synergy creates a self-steering business environment: an environment that not only reacts to anomalies in operations, but also predicts and justifies increasingly and corrects itself. Human engineers control objectives in these smart pipelines, but agentic AI systems work to achieve a new era of fault tolerant, self-healing digital commerce.

5.2.1 User Interface (UI) Layer

The user interface layer is the online front desk of a business. It's where customers interact with forms: desktop web,. mobile applications, IoT screens and API-based storefronts to headless commerce layouts. Frontend uses GraphQL or RESTful API to communicate with microservices and ensures low overhead in payloads. Schema are capable of scaling to heavy throughput architecture. Cloudflare Workers and Fastly Compute@Edge, as well as AWS Lambda@Edge, are in-edge networks standardized to support dynamic personalization before 2025. These distributed networks reduce latency by a significant extent because they execute compute near the user and offload contextual rendering (such as tailoring pricing or advice, depending on the geolocation or browsing history).

As an example, a customer in Tokyo visits a collection of products. The closest edge node translates price-specifics to the region and renders the page in milliseconds. The backend APIs continue to perform core commerce operations asynchronously. A modern UI frequently uses Progressive Web Apps (PWAs) or Single Page Applications (SPAs) based on React, SvelteKit or Next.js, which offer app-like responsiveness and offline responsiveness. Semantic search and voice-based interactions are becoming more and more enabled by the components based on the LLM, which means the user can browse the catalog by using conversational elements integrated into the frontend.

5.2.2 API Gateway and Service Mesh Layer

The traffic flowing in is centralized on one API gateway that can be seen as the point of policy and security enforcement to all client requests. The API gateway handles the following:

- **Authentication and authorization:** Using OAuth 2.0, OIDC, and JSON Web Tokens (JWTs) for stateless identity validation.
- **Rate limiting and throttling:** Managing abusive traffic and DDoS mitigation.
- **Distributed tracing:** Propagation of the W3C Trace Context headers for end-to-end observability.
- **Telemetry hooks:** Real-time request monitoring and SLA compliance metrics.

In addition to this, the Service Mesh Layer communication substrate manages east-west traffic (service-to-service). The technologies such as Istio, Linkerd, and Kuma impose service discovery, mTLS encryption, retries, and circuit breaking. Canary deployments divert a specified percentage of live traffic to new releases, whereas traffic shadowing enables performance regressions with unexposed updates to be tracked prior to production release. In one version of the payment service, the mesh logs 5 percent of live transactions into the new instance and uses distributed traces and recording latency to automatically roll back policy invocations as latency spikes.

5.2.3 Core Microservices

Microservices are representations of business capabilities in the e-commerce world. They contain a bounded context, communicate using an asynchronous message broker, such as Apache Kafka, Pulsar, or NATS, and store their data separately.

Typical services include:

- **User service:** This deals with authentication, session management, customer preferences, and loyalty programs.
- **Product catalog service:** Conducts search indexing, price change, and recommendation serving.
- **Inventory service:** Keeps an eye on quantity, warehouse synchronization, and real-time stock validity.
- **Order service/checkout service:** Plans order pipelines, such as consolidation of carts and payment arrangement.
- **Payment gateway service:** Integrates with providers such as Stripe, PayPal, or Adyen, normalizing transaction states and retries.

Auditability and replayability are ensured by event sourcing and CQRS (Command Query Responsibility Segregation) patterns, which are also essential when debugging distributed transactions.

All the microservices provide domain events—such as Order Created, Payment Authorized, and Stock Decremented—to enable other services or agentic AI subsystems to autonomously respond and ensure eventual consistency throughout the system.

5.2.4 Polyglot Databases

The *polyglot persistence* principle states that every service should choose the best database technology that fits its business load. This enhances throughput and resilience at the cost of homogenous transactional straightforwardness.

Common database allocations include these:

- **NoSQL (MongoDB, DynamoDB):** High-volume reads for catalogs and user sessions.
- **RDBMS (PostgreSQL, MySQL):** Strict transaction consistency for orders and payments.
- **Time-series (Prometheus, InfluxDB):** Metrics collection and performance analytics.
- **Graph databases (Neo4j, TigerGraph):** Relationship-driven recommendation engines.

Polyglot models enhance localized performance at the cost of fault isolation because the boundaries of data consistency are now business context-related, as opposed to systemic transactions. As a result, reliability matters due to the compensating patterns of transactions and replaying the idempotent transactions. For example, a flash sale across several warehouses can create conflicting stock updates. Kafka replay and event sourcing can reconstruct the correct inventory states after all streams converge and therefore avoid overselling and providing misinformation to customers.

5.2.5 Observability and AIOps Layer

Observability has become more of a predictive intelligence as opposed to a reactive one. In recent stacks, multi-modal telemetry is stacked, and dynamic prediction and autonomic remediation are based on AI systems.

The following aspects are part of the observability triad:

- **Metrics:** Captured via Prometheus and OpenTelemetry metrics pipelines.
- **Logs:** Centralized using Grafana Loki or Elasticsearch for high-ingest analysis.

- **Traces:** Distributed via Jaeger or Tempo, mapping causal paths across calls.

The assistants derived based on the LLM and the AIOps modules operate on these data streams. These systems cluster patterns of anomalies, summarize natural language incidents, and infer relationships of causality, which detect failing microservices, engineered based on contextual embeddings of traces and logs.

It is now possible to access automated RCA (root cause analysis) and remediation recommendations in incident dashboards on platforms such as Datadog Watchdog AI, Dynatrace Grail, and OpenAI-powered Copilots. If latency spikes in the Checkout and Payment microservices, for example, the LLM assistant interprets trace graphs, compares CPU throttling on the checkout node to regional traffic spikes, and suggests an immediate change in the scaling rule, all fully independently.

The identical AI-assisted observability basis enables agentic AI agents to execute in staging or live settings. These agents are capable of automatically restarting malfunctioning pods, isolating malfunctioning API versions, or redeploying configuration variants in real-time, reducing human effort in orders of magnitude.

5.3 Identifying Fault-Prone Microservices

The first step to predict failures in an e-commerce microservices ecosystem is to be precise; this means determining which services show the highest likelihood of failure. Fault-prone microservices are never accidental; they are a product of complicated dependencies, fatigue in operation, and changing codebases. The discovery of these risky areas has evolved out of intuition on paper to an analytical field of study with a rich amount of data, comprised of graph theory, telemetry mining, and AI-assisted context interpretation. The correct localization of the fault-prone services starts with the integration of causal inference, risk-stratified metrics, and semantic dependency graphs. The old methods of correlational prediction underrated the complexity of relations and behavior in microservice ecosystems; hence, the current research suggests that the best approaches are causal feature selection and error-type risk modeling (Mangal & Rathore, 2025 ; Phung et al., 2025).

5.3.1 Dependency Graph Analysis

Visualization is insight in distributed architectures. To maintain current service dependency graphs, AI platforms constantly construct new nodes, each representing an active microservice. To model the relationship between nodes, edges represent synchronous API calls or event streams. In the long run, these graphs evolve into running topologies of the actual runtime behavior of the system many times beyond the scope of the static architecture diagrams. Existing e-commerce systems use dynamic dependency graphs with runtime and semantic data. Every node is a microservice and every edge is a causal pathway that consists of API calls or event streams. The PageRank and Betweenness Centrally algorithms reveal high-impact nodes that transfer faults via dependency paths (Qiu et al., 2024). The flow of fault energy through topology is further explicated by the use of error-related metrics deadlocks, transaction retries, configuration drift, and the PageRank or Betweenness Centrality graph algorithms (Phung et al., 2025):

- Highly connected services serve as potential single points of failure; their downtime ripples through multiple critical paths.
- Bottleneck nodes highlight services, accumulating long latency chains or request backlogs.
- Cascading fault paths reveal cross-dependencies crucial for chaos testing and remedial isolation.

The Checkout Service concurrently interacts with the Payment, Inventory, and Order services in a massive retail platform. A network stall (or bad dependency) creates a domino effect on the downstream services. The dependency graph in this case is a diagnostic and predictive tool that will present graphical representations of the systemic stress.

5.3.2 Historical Defect and Incident Analysis

A successful prediction model is a learning tool. The pattern information concerning the operational pain points is available in tool-generated incident histories (e.g., Jira, PagerDuty, or ServiceNow). Factor analysis and regression are used to identify latent indicators of constructs of fault-proneness between object-orientation and pipeline measures. Embeddings on incident narratives also encode incident contextual variables such as configuration conflicts as risk heatmaps optimized by regression weights rather than raw frequencies.

Key indicators mined from these systems include the following:

- Incident frequency per service, showing how often each component disrupts production stability.
- Mean time between failures (MTBF), offering statistical reliability over time.
- Root cause typologies, such as configuration drift, network partitioning, and data integrity issues.

From these aggregates, risk heatmaps are generated across the microservice landscape. Teams then align high-frequency problem zones with architecture-level dependencies to derive a two-dimensional perspective where topology meets history.

A review of the past year's incidents may reveal that while Payment Service rarely fails, Inventory Service experiences frequent timeouts due to caching invalidation cycles. These insights guide prioritization for predictive monitoring and regression testing initiatives.

5.3.3 Predictive Analytics Models

After culling raw telemetry and incident patterns, machine learning pipelines transform these signals into proactive intelligence. Recent models of fault-prediction consume a mix of real-time variables and historical context to estimate the causal effect on a service of each feature and the probability of failure (Mangal, 2025). The workflow segments involve features in treatment/control states and measures mean difference in likelihood of outcomes. Attributes (e.g., commit churn, deployment frequency) are trained to be cause-effect (and so eliminate rough-set redundancy noise) to create a Neighborhood Rough-Sets Ensemble (NRSEL) (Jiang et al., 2025). The joint use of ATE-FS and NRSEL is the most interpretable and predictive, especially when the distributions of fault are imbalanced. Inventory fault probability is based on three pillars: ATE causal rank, topological centrality, and ensemble risk confidence. This provides a high-fidelity prediction that can be attributed back to its causal origins.

Some of the most commonly engineered features include the following:

- Code churn and commit frequency, measuring development volatility.
- Deployment cadence and version drift, capturing operational instability.
- Error log frequency and anomaly density, reflecting emerging degradation trends.
- Latency variance under load, indicating performance fragility.

More advanced models (gradient-boosted trees and temporal graph neural networks [GNNs]) generate dynamic risk scores. The layers of interpretability that are offered by LLM-based models enhance these scores with human-readable diagnostic statements.

Inventory Service shows a 2.1 time increase in the latency variance post-deployment, and this is similar to three earlier incidents of high latency that most probably is due to the same cause, which is indexing overhead or refreshing stale cache. This type of inference by LLMs can transform opaque predictions into operable tales to be utilized by DevOps and SRE teams. In fact, this closes the explanatory divide between data science and operations.

5.3.4 Context-Aware Log Mining

Conventional log-aggregation systems produce an enormous ocean of unstructured data that is sufficient to submerge incident responders in noise. The paradigm presents the contextual log summarization driven by the LLM and combines the semantic interpretation with time-based correlation. Based on Qiu et al. (2024), contextual prompts, such as summarizing cascading errors caused by build number 4581, are available with AI-augmented log interpretation platforms, such as Open Telemetry Copilot. LLM models associate logs with known causal features, forming time-based causal chains and removing noise. This approach reduces the MTTD through a correspondence of semantic search and causal hierarchy in the context of the feature-selection.

The key characteristics of such smart log interpreters include the following:

- Automated log triage, clustering events relevant to specific incident contexts or test failures.

- Causal sequence reconstruction, tracing how a configuration tweak led to downstream retries or circuit breaker trips.
- Conversational querying workflows, enabling engineers to ask natural language questions.

Platforms like Elastic AI Assistant and OpenTelemetry Copilot exemplify this evolution. They fuse structured observability with LLM-driven cognition to cut through complexity, decreasing mean time to detect (MTTD) and accelerating the investigative cycle.

5.4 Integrating Predictive Checks into CI/CD Pipelines

The ability to predict faults in the modern DevSecOps setting should be moved to the left as part of the continuous integration and continuous delivery (CI/CD) pipeline. This will ensure that failures are detected much earlier. Teams can build predictive code into their pipelines to make their pipelines intelligent quality gates rather than reactive executioners.

Recent advance ensemble methods such as Average Treatment Effect for Feature Selection (ATE-FS) determine feature causes and imbalance control. They make prediction explainable and operationally stable.

5.4.1 Defect Prediction Models in CI

Each commit/pull request can be seen as a code improvement as well as a risk indicator. Predictive defect models use automatic evaluation to determine the probability that any change before merge operations will cause a defect since they predict that possibility.

The models leverage factors such as the following:

- **Code complexity deltas:** Quantifying added or modified cyclomatic complexity across modules.
- **Test coverage fluctuations:** Highlighting files or branches where testing depth regresses.
- **Historical defect correlation:** Weighing prior bug density or failure frequency associated with the same developer, service, or repository.

The features that have the largest averages of the treatment effect (causal load) will receive larger impact coefficients, which provide human understandable explanations in the CI dashboards.

RGS = 0.77 means that commits contain high deployment drift (+0.15 ATE) and declining coverage (–0.10 ATE); Jenkins halts the merge and launches targeted regression testing.

A risk gate score is used to aggregate and decide whether the commit can be automatically advanced or should be paused to await further validation, such as a peer review or further testing. These approaches have been incorporated into modern CI systems, including GitHub Actions, GitLab CI, Jenkins, and Azure DevOps, through either predictive or user-written scripts. These scores are visualized in real-time using build dashboards, allowing lead engineers to discover high-risk commits and implement automated remediation processes. For example, the Payment Service has a code review score above the risk gate of 0.75, which automatically initiates another static analysis job and a focused regression suite before it is merged into a file.

5.4.2 Predictive Test Selection

Running a full regression suite on every build may be thorough, but it's also computationally expensive and time-inefficient. Predictive test selection introduces AI-driven prioritization, executing only the tests that matter most given the latest changes.

Models evaluate parameters, including these:

- **Change impact graphs:** Determining which code paths and services the commit touches.
- **Historical flaky patterns:** Identifying tests most associated with unstable failure signals.
- **Cross-service dependency matrices:** Mapping downstream services affected by code churn in the current build.

Using Bayesian inference or graph-based measures of similarity, the pipeline automatically decides which test suites are critical, usually resulting in 30-40 percent (Jiang et al., 2025) acceleration of the pipeline and no substantial reduction in the rate of fault discovery.

Using the SMOTE-NRSEL process (Jiang et al., 2025), test cases are ranked by their fault-discovery value, calculated based on synthetic data images and ensemble weights of importance. This decreases about 35 percent of the pipeline runtime and eliminates most of the unnecessary test executions without impacting recall.

For example, if a developer modifies API validation within the Order microservice, the AI model automatically throttles end-to-end payments tests and prioritizes checkout flow and inventory reservation cases instead.

5.4.3 Release Readiness Scoring

Even after successful builds and tests, deployment decisions demand measurable assurance. Predictive CI/CD systems aggregate multi-modal signals into a holistic Release Confidence Index (RCI), which is a composite metric that quantifies release stability and rollout readiness.

Components feeding the RCI include the following:

- Recent build stability rates and historical commit failure patterns
- Unresolved incident trends linked to the release branch
- Predicted failure probability from ML-based risk models
- Service health telemetry ingested directly from staging environments

When the RCI goes below a threshold, release automation systems such as Argo CD or Spinnaker automatically impose safe deployment practices, such as canary testing or blue-green rollouts, so that customers are not exposed to possible regressions.

For example, the release of a new version of the Product Catalog microservice will result in an RCI of 0.64 since the staging metrics have been showing increased response latency. The CI/CD pipeline reacts by initiating a staged deployment to 10 percent of the production traffic and gathers real-time telemetry to establish the presence of anomalies.

5.5 Targeted Testing and Anomaly Detection in Staging

The staging environment is the last testing ground in which the predictive fault management confirms system resilience prior to being deployed to the customer. In the modern dynamic microservices systems, staging is not a passive quality gateway. It is an intelligent rehearsal phase instrumented with analytics, telemetry, and automated learning. All services receive a risk tier (High/Medium/Low) according to the probability of an error (type) (Phung et al., 2025).

5.5.1 Risk-Weighted Testing

Not every microservice has an equal amount of fault exposure. Predictive systems give risk weights to single services (e.g., payment, order, inventory) and base that on aspects of transactional criticality and past failure rates. These risky services are subjected to focused chaos experiments and load testing, which put a strain on critical transactional paths. This is operationalized in modern tools such as Gremlin, LitmusChaos, and Steady Bit, which introduce network partitions, latency spikes, and partial outages to staging systems. The results of each fault-injection case shows the resilience of the architecture when the system is subjected to true-life stress to find and reinforce weak points before rolling out the production.

For example, in an international retail system, latency simulated in the Payment microservice reveals a concurrency bottleneck. Prior to release, developers fix the underlying thread pool setup that would have resulted in a defect and that would have led to extreme payment timeouts during periods of peak sales.

This is further improved by the use of ephemeral environments by infrastructure-as-code (IaC) tools like Terraform. These are cross-team, risk-free, isolated environments that can be safely scaled, as they are finite, momentary, and expressive of production.

5.5.2 Distributed Tracing and Anomaly Detection

Traditional monitoring identifies failures; distributed tracing identifies drift. State-of-the-art tracing systems are interconnected between profiling the runtime and depicting the inter-service communication baseline diagrams. For example, the mean call latency of a Cart service doubles when the deviations manifest and the anomaly detected by AI-based detection links this anomaly to the sibling services and downstream requests. When these deviations are overlaid on a live service topology, the tracing engine identifies faults occurring in one microservice node, one API endpoint, or even a single deployment version. These causal graphs speed up the root cause isolation process, which is transformed into predicting remediation instead of reacting to the incident.

In many production observability stacks, anomaly detection is implemented using seasonality-aware time-series models combined with statistical z-score thresholds or isolation forest-based outlier detection. This enables automated identification of abnormal latency or error patterns from historical telemetry.

When these signals are overlaid on a live service topology, the tracing system constructs causal dependency graphs that accelerate root-cause isolation. Instead of reacting after an outage occurs, the pipeline can move toward predictive remediation.

For example, there is an unexpected increase in the checkout latency in various nodes. The tracing tool can get an anomaly trail between the Cart API and a newer version of the Inventory service. In minutes, the defective container is reverted and normal functionality is restored.

5.5.3 Composite Metric Analysis

Individual latency indicators and CPU utilization tend to be inaccurate. To solve this, companies are using multivariate anomaly detection, which is used by algorithms that move composite signals simultaneously:

- Latency variations coupled with error-rate fluctuations
- API call graph distortions paired with request drop patterns
- Resource utilization metrics aggregated across multi-region clusters

This form of composite analysis is provoked by either unsupervised learning or time outlier models to distinguish between local mishaps (e.g., a spike of one node) and system-wide mishaps (referred to many regions). This wholistic approach improves credibility and minimizes false positives, particularly in regionally scaled architectures and cloud-native settings.

5.5.4 Continuous Observability Dashboards

The days of personalized stationary dashboards are long gone. The existing observability suites—Grafana Cloud, Dynatrace Davis AI, and Datadog Watchdog—offer real-time self-adaptive visualizations with embedded reasoning engine and LLM layers.

Dashboards continually highlight:

- Emerging anomaly clusters across services
- Temporal failure correlations among deployments
- Auto-generated RCA (root cause analysis) narratives

As an example, assume that there was a spike in API latency in the Payments API under the Redis cache eviction following the configuration update in release 12.4.7. The visualization does not simply report the symptom, it reports the cause and initiates a correction immediately. MTTR is decreased to a great extent.

5.6 Measuring Business and Operational Impact

Predictive fault management is measurably beneficial in terms of business continuity and efficiency in engineering. According to adoption of ATE-FS and NRSEL, ensembles require statistically validated uplifts across industrial benchmarks (Jiang et al., 2025).

5.6.1 Cutting Down on Failures

By incorporating risk gates and predictive monitoring driven by AI into CI/CD pipelines, critical failures are reduced by 40 to 60 percent. An early anomaly absorption prevents cascading failures from escalating into failures and boosts user trust and conversion stability at sales peaks.

5.6.2 Improved Mean Time to Repair (MTTR)

The time of incident analysis is reduced to minutes with the help of RCA based on LLM. Engineers do not have to search through thousands of logs, and instead are presented with causally ordered summaries of events, together with hints on how they can be remediated and likely root causes.

5.6.3 Operational Efficiency

Predictive gates and targeted testing reduce the amount of work done in the testing by 30-50 percent, which allows manual efforts to be concentrated in the areas of innovation and architectural development instead of time spent doing repetitive regression work.

5.6.4 Continuous Learning Feedback Loop

Prior resolved instances deliver retroactive telemetry and tagged insights into predictive models in a self-evolving reliability loop. Throughout these cycles, the system becomes more familiar with weaker signals, gradually lowering the number of false negatives and increasing resilience.

5.7 Conclusion

Speculation of faults in e-commerce pipelines of microservices is a combination of architectural rigor and AI thought and sight. Combining predictive modeling, adaptive testing, and agentic observability through CI/CD ecosystems will enable organizations to achieve the last dream of DevOps, which is the resilience at scale. Architecture maturity is in its capacity to foresee and act and recover. The existing e-commerce systems are transforming reliability into a preventative factor and not a living and breathing element by predictively detecting faults, using AI-enhanced testing, and continuously learning. This enables customers to have a sense of trust despite the invisibility and complexity of such systems.

CHAPTER 6

Security Implications and DevSecOps Alignment

Reliability and security are two sides of a coin in current day DevSecOps ecosystems. Flaws in microservices are not only a possible reliability problem but are also latent security vulnerabilities. Fault prediction in the paradigm of smart DevSecOps does not only assist teams in creating systems that are more stable, but it also helps them create systems that are safer. When we examine the modules that are prone to faults—modules with a history of high error rates, frequent rollbacks, or recurring bug reports—what we find are the very vulnerabilities that threat actors are seeking. Faults and vulnerabilities have the same heritage in that they are complex, difficult to maintain, and have irregular dependencies and visibility.

6.1 How Fault-Prone Modules Map to Security Risks

When we analyze fault-prone modules against those with a history of high error rates, frequent rollbacks, or recurring bug reports, we're often uncovering the same weak points that threat actors look for. Faults and vulnerabilities share a common ancestry: complexity, poor maintainability, inconsistent dependencies, and lack of visibility.

D. Sharma and A. Syed, *Fault Detection in Microservice Architectures*,
https://doi.org/10.1007/979-8-8688-2712-9_6

For example:

- Services that fail with the help of the null reference exceptions might not be input-validated; therefore, they can be subject to injection attacks.
- Modules that experience constant churn and have hotfixes are usually not properly tested, and they provide unmonitored code paths where exploits can lurk.

Mapping fault-proneness to security exposure can help DevSecOps teams move toward no longer patching vulnerabilities but protecting against them. They can focus on potential problematic areas in advance, before vulnerabilities are ever detected by a security scanner or a malicious attacker. Threat intelligence, in turn, is an internal source of fault prediction and is generated right through operational signals. As an example, a module that fails frequently with null reference exceptions or bad data indicates more structural vulnerability. Such weakness frequently intersects with a lack of input validation or authentication.

Likewise, objects that are constantly in churn or are susceptible to quick hotfixes are likely to have code paths that are not well tested, and hence provide blind spots where vulnerabilities can reside.

Fault-proneness to security exposure mapping can enable DevSecOps teams to transform into reactive security. Predictive analytics determine the location of a potential risk as opposed to the vulnerabilities being realized by scanners or attackers. Basically, fault prediction is a different category of threat intelligence: a self-generated one.

6.1.1 API Vulnerabilities

The API is the main communication meshwork of a microservices architecture and at the same time one of the most frequent sources of functional failures and security vulnerabilities. An API with a bad habit of generating spikes of 4xx/5xx responses on a rate basis, breach of contracts, or breakage of integrations, is a red flag of a possible security vulnerability.

To illustrate this, a recurring pattern of log 400 Bad requests or 500 Internal Server errors shows not only bad business code, but bad input validation, bad schema enforcement, or bad parsing code. The same weaknesses provide opportunities to injection attacks, deserialization attacks, or buffer vulnerabilities. Such trends are automatically identified in a DevSecOps setting that is driven by fault prediction. On seeing an API endpoint with increasing fault probability due to recent commits, the analytics system may issue an alert that can be used to automatically perform dynamic scanning, fuzz testing, or contract validation before being promoted to production.

In addition to point-in-time detection, fault prediction can be used to detect behavioral drift in APIs. Under the conditions of newer versions acting inconsistently with already existing contracts, client integrations fail and attackers take note. The use of predictive monitoring helps security tests keep pace with functional changes and detect authentication failures, token mismanagement, or data leakage as early as possible in the development lifecycle.

6.1.2 Misconfigurations

Some of the most devastating security breaches in contemporary infrastructure are attributed to configuration errors. A poorly set up S3 bucket, an exposed port in Kubernetes, or a lax IAM policy can reverse years of rigorous engineering. Interestingly, a lot of misconfigurations present initially as a service failing to start, connection refused, or certificate mismatch.

Misconfigurations are also one of the most influential causes of current breaches, not only of exposed S3 buckets but also of lax IAM permissions. These problems can manifest themselves initially as technical malfunctions, such as a failed attempt to start the service, refusal to connect, and certificate errors.

Fault prediction enhances security posture by:

- Flagging components with frequent configuration failures for pre-release security audits.
- Automating guardrail checks (e.g., encryption validation, policy enforcement) whenever misconfiguration-prone modules are updated.
- Correlating configuration fault patterns with known breach vectors to prioritize hardening efforts.

By correlating configuration-related faults with security posture, teams can build automated guardrails. For example, if a service deployment fails due to missing environment variables or misaligned permissions, the DevSecOps pipeline can automatically invoke policy checks. Fault prediction enhances this by identifying services that frequently fail due to configuration issues, marking them as candidates for deeper security auditing. See Table 6-1.

Table 6-1. *Mapping Misconfiguration Faults to Security Implications*

Manifestation	Operational Fault	Security Implication
Service start	Failed service start due to missing variables	Potential exposure of environment secrets or fallback to insecure defaults
Connectivity	Connection refused or certificate mismatches	Misaligned permissions or encryption policies
Access control	Denied connections	Overly permissive or broken IAM roles

In smart DevSecOps pipelines, misconfiguration detection becomes continuous. Fault-prediction models trained on historical deployment logs can proactively flag "misconfiguration-prone" components, prompting automated verification of permissions, encryption policies, and access controls before the next release.

6.1.3 Dependency Risks

Modern applications are constructed based on a web of dependencies—open-source libraries, in-house frameworks, and third-party services. There are risk profiles associated with each dependency. The modules whose faults are highly dependency-dependent are especially concerning: the same instability as that of version conflicts or runtime errors can conceal the existence of unpatched vulnerabilities.

Another example is a microservice that is not consistently available due to a dependency version mismatch. It can also be lagging behind significant security updates. This is because these modules can be detected as faulty early enough. Automated dependency scans (like Snyk or Dependency-Track) should be performed prior to deployment.

Such dependency instability-security exposure correlation may significantly break DevSecOps teams. They can focus on patching and code review based on severity, or on a risk of future failure or exploitability.

6.2 Embedding Fault Prediction into Security Gates

Traditional security gates in CI/CD pipelines initiate compliance and prevent known vulnerabilities before production. These gates are, however, normally reactive—they attend to what has been discovered. They are proactive, with the fault prediction incorporated.

A fault-aware pipeline attributes to each build or module a predicted fault score based on its churn, past test outcomes, past incidents, dependency change behavior, and configuration change behavior. This score is compared to some value, and, if it rises, the pipeline will close its security gates by default:

- **Enhanced analysis:** Triggering additional SAST/DAST scans, API fuzzing, or contract testing against high-risk services
- **Mandatory review:** Requiring peer review, security sign-off, or threat modeling sessions before merge approval
- **Deep scanning:** Enforcing comprehensive image and dependency scans, stricter policy-as-code validations, or container runtime security checks

This adaptive gating ensures that attention and resources are directed where they're most needed. It also prevents overburdening teams with unnecessary checks on stable components.

How it works:

1. The fault-prediction model continuously learns based on the history of commits, test results, incident reports, and operational information.
2. In CI/CD, the fault of each module is estimated.
3. Once the score exceeds a given threshold, the system implements a stricter level of security validation.
4. The result of such checks is applied as inputs into the model in order to enhance past predictions.

A unified fault-prediction system that runs against DevSecOps gates enables organizations to develop an autopiloting data-driven defense system that is smarter with every deployment.

6.3 Proactive Mitigation: Automated Policies and SRE Handoff

DevSecOps teams must transform forecasts into automated mitigation measures to effectively impact fault analytics.

6.3.1 Automated Policy Enforcement

Through policy-as-code frameworks (like Open Policy Agent or Kyverno), fault prediction can trigger automatic enforcement mechanisms. For instance:

- In the case of a high-risk module, the policy engine can block deployment until it passes the regression and security tests.
- If the dependency instability leads to an increase in fault risk, the system will automatically freeze the version of the module and request a patch review.
- Well-known APIs are automatically sandboxed in staging environments to further test fault-prone modules.

This type of automated enforcement lowers human error and minimizes the mean time to detect (MTTD) vulnerabilities. More to the point, it ensures that predictive intelligence becomes an active component of the security organization.

6.3.2 The SRE Connection

SRE (site reliability engineers) are the building blocks of contemporary software delivery. By incorporating fault prediction into their toolchain, SRE teams can determine where failure is likely to happen before it occurs.

When predictive models flag high-risk modules, SRE teams can:

- **Increase observability:** Adding targeted metrics, log collection, and alerts around flagged services
- **Prepare playbooks:** Developing incident response procedures with specific recovery actions for anticipated failure modes
- **Test recovery:** Executing rollback procedures and simulating fault conditions before production incidents occur

This collaboration of DevSecOps and SRE fills this gap of forecast, deterrence, and reaction.

SREs can also react faster to these incidences and provide beneficial information regarding the operation process to the fault-prediction model. This process improves over time, as the feedback is continuous.

6.3.3 Self-Healing Systems

Full deployment of smart DevSecOps by means of automation and AI leads to self-healing behaviors. Self-healing systems can identify known faults and anomalies in the module. Then they can:

- Automatically roll back the deployment.
- Reroute traffic to a stable version.
- Trigger container restarts or policy-driven reconfigurations.
- Elevate monitoring and apply temporary rate limits, feature flags, or access controls until the risk is mitigated.

This proactive remediation ensures that small faults never escalate into widespread outages or breaches. Over time, these self-correcting patterns become an integral part of the organization's resilience strategy.

6.4 Cultural Alignment: Developers, Security Engineers, and Operations

Culture can be the source of maintaining alignment, but technology can help do this as well. The cooperation between development, security, and operations is not merely a requirement that smart DevSecOps survives on.

6.4.1 Developers: Shifting Left with Insight

Fault prevention is the frontline for developers. They can act early by integrating the insights of fault prediction in their day-to-day activities, either via dashboards, IDE extensions, or pull request summaries. Once a developer discovers that their recent code extensions have increased the risk of a probable fault in a module, the system creates an immediate feedback loop of improvement. This is what shift-left security implies: quality and security in the hands of the developers. Rather than considering it a burden of compliance, security is perceived as a natural extension of code discipline.

6.4.2 Security Engineers: Prioritization Through Data

Fault prediction serves as an effective prioritization window to security groups. They do not need to scan all the components evenly; instead, they can scan the ones statistically more likely to go bad or be exploited. This results in improved use of resources and quicker vulnerability patching.

Predictive analytics will also assist in resolving the communication gap between the engineers and the executives. Quantified and data-driven risk models can convert technical weakness into business consequence, which can be measured. This means more informed decision-making as to where to allocate security efforts.

6.4.3 Operations: Building Predictive Resilience

Predictive insights give operations teams and SREs in particular the ability to plan capacity, strengthen configurations, and build runbooks that are more resilient. They also plan the occurrences ahead of time rather than responding to them as they happen, based on anticipatory indications.

Silos are broken when Dev, Sec, and Ops have a common understanding of the areas where risks and faults are most likely to occur. All people operate on a common predictive map of system fragility.

6.4.4 The Human Factor

Trust and transparency are the final elements of predictive DevSecOps. Models should be articulable. In other words, teams should be able to make sense of why a module is considered risky. This openness creates trust and cooperation. When engineers have confidence in the recommendations of the system, predictive analytics become a base of decision-making.

6.5 Toward a Predictive Security Culture

Fault prediction is not a technological addition. In fact, the incorporation of the fault prediction into DevSecOps is a culture development. It transforms security as a part of response mechanism to a predictive-based practice that is based on data and constant learning. Fault-prone modules can assist organizations in identifying risks before they occur. They do this by assuming that the fault-prone modules represent the manifestation of the underlying weaknesses. Once they include those insights in automated gates and SRE operations, they can act decisively. And when teams are oriented to anticipating intelligence, they establish a culture of active resilience. All logs, commits, and deployments are not a signal, just an artifact of operation in smart DevSecOps. Something that can be learned, put in action, and make the whole ecosystem stronger. The future of safe and trustworthy microservice is not responsive to failure, but active and dynamic, converting uncertainty into knowledge. It is the knowledge that leads to safety.

6.6 Conclusion

This chapter has established that fault-prone modules can be regarded as a strong indicator of security exposure and that fault prediction can be integrated into DevSecOps practices to make security a data-driven and continuous process. By using operational fragility and vulnerability risk correlation across APIs, configurations, and dependencies, organizations can provide an internal threat intelligence capability based on organizational systems. Predictive insights are then converted into tangible protective measures through automated policy enforcement, dynamic security gates, and collaboration between SREs, and these practices are maintained with time through cultural alignment between Dev, Sec, and Ops.

Yet the techniques explored here represent only the foundation. The machine learning models referenced throughout this chapter—classifiers that score fault probability, anomaly detectors that flag behavioral drift, and policy engines that enforce risk-based gates—deserve deeper examination. How exactly do these models learn from telemetry? Which architectures best capture the temporal, spatial, and relational patterns inherent in microservice behavior? How can organizations move beyond threshold-based alerts toward a truly predictive, self-healing infrastructure?

The next chapter will address these questions directly. It begins by examining the machine learning foundations that underpin fault prediction tree-based ensembles, support vector machines, and reinforce probabilistic models before progressing to deep learning architectures capable of capturing complex temporal sequences (LSTM, GRU) and service dependency structures (Graph Neural Networks). The chapter then explores how neural networks enable sophisticated anomaly detection through autoencoders and hybrid architectures, how predictive analytics can optimize resource allocation and prevent saturation-driven failures, and how real-time monitoring with Prometheus and Grafana operationalizes these models at scale.

Most significantly, Chapter 7 examines the emerging frontier of self-healing systems and AIOps, where fault prediction, security awareness, and automated remediation converge into an autonomous infrastructure that's capable of detecting, diagnosing, and resolving issues without human intervention. The chapter concludes with the research challenges that remain: managing data drift through automated retraining, preserving privacy via federated learning, deploying models to resource-constrained edge environments, securing ML pipelines themselves under zero-trust principles, and the nascent field of agentic AI for autonomous security operations.

PART IV

Advanced Directions and Frameworks

CHAPTER 7

Advanced Fault Prediction and DevSecOps Integration

7.1 Introduction: From Fault Detection to Predictive Resilience

Microservice architectures are dynamic; they comprise hundreds of loosely named services, with their respective deployment schedule, metrics, and dependence. Faults are now no longer caused by any one failure point; they cascade through service chains that are usually obscured by volatile anomalies.

Predictive resilience uses fault detection in a learning field in a continuous manner. Within DevSecOps, it unites:

- **Development:** Feeding fault analytics back into design and code reviews
- **Security:** Treating every fault signal as a possible security symptom
- **Operations:** Automating recovery and capacity decisions

The goal is no longer just to *find* faults but to *forecast, mitigate, and self-heal* before end users feel the impact.

D. Sharma and A. Syed, *Fault Detection in Microservice Architectures*,
https://doi.org/10.1007/979-8-8688-2712-9_7

7.2 Machine Learning Foundations for Fault Prediction

Machine learning provides a more realistic basis for fault prediction in microservices compared to classical statistical models. Classical linear and logistic regression presuppose that the predictors affect the result in independent and approximately linear ways, which is rarely the case when all of the aspects of latency, queue depth, memory pressure, GC pauses, and thread contention co-evolve and affect each other. In contrast, modern ML approaches treat fault prediction as a supervised learning task in high-dimensional telemetry. They learn complex decision limits directly from the data without making strong parametric models.

At a high level, a fault-prediction pipeline in microservices has four conceptual steps. First, raw observability data measures, such as logs and traces, are transformed into feature vectors—this includes windowed means of latency percentiles, error rates, saturation, dependency fan-out, and graph-structure traces-based features. Second, this labeled data is collected through incident history or fault injection. Fault injection itself may label healthy and faulty examples and may include more finer-grained labels like fault type and faulty microservice. Third, trained ML models highlight the difference between these classes; they are cross-validated to prevent overfitting. Lastly, the trained model determines continuous scores on fresh telemetry at runtime to generate early-warning signals regarding latent errors.

7.2.1 Key ML Families

Key ML families include:

1. **Tree-based ensembles (XGBoost, LightGBM, Random Forest)**

   Tree-based ensembles create a practical foundation of most fault-prediction systems since they are a trade-off between accuracy, robustness, and interpretability. Random Forests, XGBoost, and LightGBM, among other algorithms, can be trained to learn nonlinear decision surfaces consisting of a large number of shallow decision trees that cover distinct features of the feature space.

From a microservices perspective, tree ensembles offer several advantages:

- **Nonlinear interaction captures:** They naturally model interactions such as "high p99 latency AND growing queue depth AND elevated downstream error rate" as a specific branch in a tree, without feature engineering cross-terms by hand.
- **Heterogeneous feature handling:** They ingest a mix of continuous metrics (CPU, memory, latency) and categorical attributes (service name, region, deployment ring) with minimal preprocessing.
- **Built-in importance and attribution:** Feature importance scores, gain statistics, and SHAP-style attributions provide operators with insight into why a prediction was made, which is essential for root-cause analysis and for building trust in automated signals.

Empirical research on microservice fault tolerance is highly consistent and prove that gradient boosting variants like these work. Since XGBoost and LightGBM have high macro-F1s and good precision-recall trade-offs, rendering them is especially useful during the early-stage fault prediction, when false negatives are expensive.

Sometimes tree models are combined with deep sequence models, with the trees serving as discontinuous, frontend, pattern detectors. They are fast and interpretable and hand over ambiguous patterns or longer-horizon patterns to recurrent systems.

2. **Support Vector Machines (SVM)**

Another classical but still applicable group of models are Support Vector Machines (SVMs). SVMs in their simplest form are trained to learn a hyperplane between healthy and poorly fitting states in a high-dimensional feature space, which maximizes the distance between the two classes. By introducing kernel functions, SVMs implicitly project features into even higher dimensional spaces, enabling the model to form nonlinear boundaries without any explicit nonlinear features.

In operational terms, SVMs can be effective when:

- The feature space is neither too large nor too small, and it is very informative (e.g., log-derived features or statistics of traces at a level of detail). Classes are somewhat separable but can have curved edges (e.g., having a distinction within instead of degrading throughput regimes).
- The training data is not huge. At very large scales, regular training SVMs can be costly. This is alleviated by linear and approximate variants.

  Microservice operations teams may use the SVMs as small discriminators when labels are fairly clean and resource budgets are tight.

  They serve as reference points in research systems that are eventually transitioned into ensembles or deep models. They are also appealing with controlled systems like individual clusters or known behavior critical services.

3. **Naïve Bayes and probabilistic models**

   Simple Bayesian networks and Markov-like models are probabilistic models, and they fill a useful microservice fault-prediction niche. Naive Bayes assumes conditional feature independence under the label of the class, a premise that is clearly broken in complex systems. However, it can still get quite impressive results on some of the subproblems. A benign warning or fault related text (log anomaly classification) is an instance of an advantage of Naive Bayes since it is easy and can operate on sparse and dimensional text representations.

   More patterned probabilistic models are further generalized by modeling explicitly temporal and state transitions. The system can be represented by Markov chain models, hidden Markov models, and their variations. They learn transition probabilities on historical traces between states (e.g., normal, degraded, near-failure, failed) and telemetry sequences. After training, such models support:

- **Short-horizon failure probability estimation:** Given the current state and recent observations, they estimate the likelihood of entering a failure state within a future time window.
- **Scenario reasoning:** Evaluating "what-if" transitions, such as the effect of prolonged high load on entering a degraded state.

Probabilistic models do not perform as well as ensembles and deep networks on raw data. They are superior in interpretability and can be incorporated into a bigger decision structure.

As an example, a Markov model can be used to estimate the rough state of an organization as an input into a higher capacity ML model or as a sanity check on more opaque predictors.

4. **Foundation guide: XGBoost**

XGBoost is a highly productive code of gradient-boosted decision-trees and one of the most useful starting coding languages on microservice ecosystem fault prediction. It constructs a group of shallow trees sequentially where each successive tree is centered on the remaining error of the former trees and the tree successively tightens the decision boundary between normal and faulty states by correcting the errors of the prior trees. It is particularly applied to those cases, where the nonlinear relationships are also known among the code measures, CI events and runtime telemetry that would not be analyzed through a simple threshold, or linear model. Paying attention to its operational characteristics,

XGBoost best fits the description of a supervised binary or multiclass fault likelihoods supervised classifier. There are common groups of features: static (complexity, churn, ownership) and CI/CD (test failures, lint violations, my security scan results), and runtime (error rates, p95/p99, latency, CPU use, memory use) features. Trained on historic events and defect labels, this model gives predictions which are adjusted to provide guidance e.g. likely to introduce defect with probability 0.78, which DevSecOps teams can then rely on to provide a gate on defenses pulling deployments, prioritize reviews or other testing phases.

7.2.2 Recommended Configuration and Training Pattern

The following setup provides a fair starting point when it comes to fault-prediction activities:

- **Both expressiveness and risk of overfitting give rise to max depth:** When max depth = 6, this is the point where the tree stops growing and is no longer extended.
- **learning_rate = 0.1:** This is the rate at which an individual tree corrects past mistakes; the intermediate values tend to work very well in practice.
- **n_estimators = 300:** The abundance of trees will be enabled to ensure the use of sufficient others and the learning rate will filter the over-fitting, which can then be adjusted down or applied together with early stopping.
- **subsample = 0.8:** Use overall performance and generalization in the presence of noisy data, which is an enhancement of random sampling/randomly selected rows of a tree on the subsample.

A typical workflow is as follows:

1. Dependency installation involving XGBoost, scikit-learn, and Pandas dependencies.
2. Prepare and train X and Y based on curated telemetry/labels (e.g., build health vs. build regression).
3. Instantiate XGBClassifier with the previous hyperparameters.
4. Fit and test on a holdout set, then adjust thresholds (e.g., taking 0.7 as the threshold to a high-risk build).

In fully trained models, a validation set is used by a team to introduce early stopping in order to minimize training time and avoid overfitting. It does this by stopping the training when further inclusion of additional trees does not improve performance.

In a DevSecOps pipeline, XGBoost works well. It creates a quality and risk gate, which is triggered once the common build and statical checks have been completed, but after the broad rollout is not triggered.

- **Stage 1:** Build, unit tests, static analysis, SAST/DAST, and dependency scanning run as usual
- **Stage 2:** Feature extraction step aggregates:
    - Code-level signals (diff size, touched files, ownership, churn)
    - CI signals (test failures, flakiness, security findings count)
    - Historical context (service incident history, past defect density)
- **Stage 3:** The XGBoost model scores the build or commit and outputs a fault likelihood
- **Stage 4:** The pipeline policy reacts to the score, for example
    - If the predicted defect probability > 0.7, additional peer reviews, expanded test suites, or canary-only deployment is recommended.
    - If probability is moderate (e.g., 0.4–0.7), allow deployment but automatically tighten observability. This means lower alert thresholds, more aggressive anomaly detection, and shorter rollback decision windows.
    - If risk is low, continue with the normal deployment path.

This pattern does not take the place of predictive modeling. a smart prioritization layer makes XGBoost smarter. Risky changes are vetted and assume more defensive runtime postures, whereas low-risk changes are permitted to pass through the pipeline.

Several practical considerations improve the reliability and maintainability of an XGBoost-based fault predictor in production:

- **Class imbalance handling:** Faults are very rare and class techniques like class weight, focal losses, or positive oversampling may be used to achieve a large increase in the recall of true faults.
- **Feature stability:** Automatically and periodically examine definitions of features as services are refactored.
- **Explainability:** Periodically review feature definitions as the services are refactored. Observability schemas will keep on evolving, and stale or drifting features will become more and more problematic to the performance of models over time.

- **Retraining cadence:** Surface feature importance/SHAP-like explanations explain why a build was marked and allowed to be failed (e.g., uncharacteristically high code churn and recent test failures in a historically sensitive service).
- **Introduce retraining:** Retraining is introduced into CI/CD (once a week or once a month) with newly labeled builds and incidents so that the model will track the changing architecture and coding patterns.

By using XGBoost as a native decision-making element in the DevSecOps platform, companies can transform historical data regarding defects and incidents into a constantly enhancing predictive control, moving quality assurance and security posture to a more proactive risk-management approach than a reactive defect discovery one.

7.3 Deep Learning Architectures for Fault Modeling

Deep learning models overcome the constraints of classical machine learning and tree-based ensembles to the extent that they can learn hierarchical feature representations and temporal, spatial, and structural patterns that emerge naturally out of training data. In the same way that classical approaches involve feature engineering, computing windowed aggregates, correlation coefficients, or interaction terms, deep neural networks automatically learn these transformations. Deep learning architectures frequently find patterns that human engineers would have failed to notice. This characteristic in microservices fault prediction corresponds to models with a view to subtle system dynamics: the spread of latency degradation in dependent services, the progression of error cascades in minutes, and the presentation of resource contention by multidimensional telemetry.

7.3.1 Architectural Families and Their Specializations

Convolutional Neural Networks (CNNs)

CNNs are outstanding at learning spatial patterns or finding correlations and structures in multidimensional input spaces. Spatial structure is inherent to microservices telemetry: metrics of related services (payment service, fraud detection service, ledger service) are correlated when the system is under stress. The CPU, memory, and network measurements of a single host correlate.

CNNs use convolutional filters, which scan through the dimensions of the inputs and learn to identify meaningful patterns (e.g., sudden synchronous spikes in several metrics), which is a sign of coordinated resource contention, or gradual degradation patterns in batch processing windows. The pooling layers combine information within local areas, and invariance to small timing differences and metric scaling differences is constructed.

Practical microservices applications include:

- **Learning anomaly detection in the correlation matrix (between services):** 2D spatial structure of a pair-wise correlation matrix between services and detecting anomalies in the correlation patterns before failures with CNNs.
- **Multi-sensor integration:** Combining metrics from infrastructure (CPU, memory, I/O), application (request latency, GC time, thread pools), and network (packet loss, jitter, bandwidth) into a single multi-channel input, with CNNs learning how these channels interact.
- **Log embedding visualization:** The projection of log sequences into dense vectors and CNN to identify abnormal "shapes" in the embedding space.

Recurrent Neural Networks and Long Short-Term Memory (LSTM)

RNNs preserve the hidden state through the time steps that make them capture the sequential dependencies and time dynamics. Although the vanilla RNN architecture is conceptually simple, it has the issue of gradient vanishing and gradient explosion when sequences are long, which restricts practical horizons to several time steps (around 10-50).

Long short-term memory (LSTM) networks overcome this issue with the help of gating. Input gates regulate whether new information is added to the cell state, forget gates enable selective forgetting of old information, and output gates regulate which information is passed to the next layer. This architecture allows LSTMs to remember the relevant context of sequences of hundreds of time steps; which is important in microservices where fault precursors can take minutes to hours before failure is evident.

In fault-prediction contexts, LSTM models typically operate on windowed time-series data:

- **Input:** Sequences of metric vectors at fixed time intervals (e.g., 60 seconds of one-minute-aggregated metrics, yielding a 60 × 50 tensor where 50 is the metric dimension).
- **Hidden layers:** One or more LSTM layers learning temporal patterns and dependencies, often with dropout for regularization.
- **Output:** Binary (healthy vs. faulty) or multiclass (fault type) classification, or regression predicting time-to-failure.

The LSTM's capacity to capture variable-length temporal context makes it particularly effective for the following:

- **Early fault detection:** Learning that certain sequences of metric changes precede failure by 5-30 minutes, enabling proactive remediation.
- **Fault type classification:** Different fault modes exhibit characteristic temporal signatures (e.g., memory leaks show gradual growth, connection pool exhaustion shows abrupt saturation), which LSTMs can learn to discriminate.
- **Anomaly detection:** Deviations from learned normal temporal patterns trigger alerts without requiring explicit threshold specification.

Transformer and Attention-Based Models

Transformers add multi-head attention capabilities that allow models to attend to multiple aspects of the input sequence, with each head training to focus on a different temporal relationship or feature interaction. Transformers, unlike RNNs, operate on whole sequences in parallel (the nature of RNNs is sequential, and therefore hard to parallelize), and improve the training of long sequences by many orders of magnitude.

In the context of microservices fault prediction, the transformer has specific advantages when working with:

- **Large-scale event logs:** Handling thousands of individual events of multiple services in order without them being summarized into fixed-dimensional aggregates, keeping detailed timing and causality data.
- **Multi-service traces:** Learning to weigh inter-service dependencies through their predictive usefulness by modeling the causal relationships between events across service boundaries.
- **Variable-length contexts:** Since it is a natural property of transformers that input length is variable (not fixed, as with CNNs or RNNs), they naturally respond to incidents with different characteristic timescales.

7.3.2 Foundation Guide for LSTM for Time-Series Fault Forecasting

LSTM networks have a convenient accessible point to deep learning-based fault prediction. The following example illustrates a simple though practical implementation that can be developed and tested. The production deployments of such applications follow the same patterns, just on a larger scale.

```
#Environment Setup:
pip install tensorflow numpy pandas scikit-learn
#Model Architecture and Training:
from tensorflow.keras.models import Sequential
from tensorflow.keras.layers import LSTM, Dense, Dropout
from tensorflow.keras.optimizers import Adam
import numpy as np

# Assume X_train shape: (num_samples, time_steps, num_features)
# e.g., (1000, 60, 50) = 1000 sequences of 60 time steps, 50 metrics each
# Assume y_train shape: (1000,) with binary labels (0=healthy, 1=faulty)

model = Sequential([
    LSTM(64, input_shape=(window_size, num_features), return_
    sequences=True),
    Dropout(0.2),
```

```
    LSTM(32, return_sequences=False),
    Dropout(0.2),
    Dense(16, activation='relu'),
    Dense(1, activation='sigmoid')
])

model.compile(
    optimizer=Adam(learning_rate=0.001),
    loss='binary_crossentropy',
    metrics=['accuracy', 'AUC']
)

history = model.fit(
    X_train, y_train,
    epochs=30,
    batch_size=64,
    validation_split=0.2,
    verbose=1
)
```

Key design considerations include:

- **Two stacked LSTM layers:** The first layer with `return_sequences=True` passes full sequences to the second layer, enabling the model to learn hierarchical temporal features. The second LSTM aggregates the entire sequence into a single representation.
- **Dropout regularization:** After each LSTM layer, this prevents overfitting, a particular concern when training on limited historical failure examples.
- **Dense hidden layer:** It provides additional nonlinearity before the final binary classification output with sigmoid activation.
- **Binary cross-entropy loss:** This is appropriate for binary fault classification. For multi-class problems (e.g., different fault types), use `categorical_crossentropy`.

```
# Generate predictions on new (streaming) telemetry windows
predictions = model.predict(X_test)  # shape: (num_test_samples, 1)

# predictions[i, 0] is a probability between 0 and 1
# 0 = high confidence in healthy state
# 1 = high confidence in faulty/degraded state
# 0.5 = maximum uncertainty

# Interpretation patterns:
# Rising predicted probability: system entering degradation, recommend
proactive scaling or diagnostics
# Steady high probability: sustained fault condition, escalate to incident
response
# Flattened signal near 0: stable healthy operation, normal
monitoring posture
# Rapid transitions: abrupt state changes, potential trigger for
immediate alerts
```

Operational Deployment Pattern

In a production environment, LSTM inference is typically integrated into monitoring stacks as follows:

```
# Create custom Prometheus metric for LSTM predictions
fault_probability = pc.Gauge(
    'microservice_fault_probability',
    'LSTM-predicted probability of fault within next 5 minutes',
    labelnames=['service_name', 'region', 'deployment_ring']
)

# In your monitoring collection loop:
for service in monitored_services:
    recent_metrics = fetch_recent_metrics(service, window=60)  # 60 minutes
    X = preprocess_and_normalize(recent_metrics)
    prob = model.predict(X[np.newaxis, :, :], verbose=0)[0, 0]
```

```
    fault_probability.labels(
        service_name=service.name,
        region=service.region,
     deployment_ring=service.ring
  ).set(prob)
```

This pushes LSTM prediction outputs into Prometheus as a custom metric, making them available for the following:

- Trends of fault probability generated in Grafana dashboards in real-time.
- Rule based alerts, which are incident responses initiated when the likelihood of a fault exceeds 0.7 in five minutes.
- Automated remediation, which launches self-healing or AIOps operations on threshold violation.
- Post-incident analysis is the relationship between LSTM signals and the occurrence of actual incidences to maximize model training.

The practical usefulness of deep learning fault prediction is not based on the accuracy of the model itself, but on strict interconnection with the operational processes.

Prometheus Integration Pattern

- The LSTM model is continuously running, where recent metrics are processed either through custom Python exporter or a sidecar container.
- Prometheus metrics (a gauge, histogram or counter type, depending on the signal) are predictions.
- Prometheus scrapes excavations on typical time intervals (e.g., every 30 seconds).
- Grafana shows visualization of trends of prediction, and it shows the times when high fault probability occurs.
- Prometheus alerting rules operate based on sustained high-probabilities.

- The use of alert firing is combined with incident management systems, automatic remediation processes, or direct on-call notifications.

Other techniques include:

- **Adaptive thresholding:** Comparing recent baseline metrics to normalize predictions and taking into account the heterogeneity of systems (what is considered a high risk on one service is considered a low risk on a different service)
- **Ensemble approaches:** Predicting with LSTMs and with tree-based models and probabilistic baselines, the ensemble members are weighted by their past performance on the particular service.
- **Hierarchical models:** Training distinct LSTMs to different service levels or failure modes (e.g., latency based failures vs. throughput-based failures).

7.3.3 Practical Considerations for Production Deployment

Deep learning models introduce operational challenges beyond classical algorithms:

- **Inference latency:** LSTM inference running on a GPU can be fast (in milliseconds), but on a CPU it can take hundreds of milliseconds. The deployment of production involves the strategy of resource allocation and batching so that the monitoring system doesn't become a bottleneck.
- **Model versioning:** Deep learning models are vulnerable to hyperparametric changes, training data structures, and input normalization. Institute version keeping, A/B testing model versions, and rollback capabilities when newer model versions impact operational performance.
- **Retraining complexity:** The retraining of LSTM models can be more stable than tree models, which can be retrained every day. Install retraining pipelines that are automated with meticulous validation gates to block deployment of models that degenerate on holdout test sets.

- **Explainability:** LSTM results, known to be generally reliable, are infamously hard to interpret. Additive prediction augmented with attention visualization (or any SHAP-like feature attribution) demonstrate the time windows that most affected the prediction.

Companies that have used deep learning to predict faults in microservices have a common pattern where they initially deploy LSTM models on one service or one type of fault, build a robust training and deployment model infrastructure, and finally scale to the next service and fault mode. This intended adoption reduces the operational risk and creates skills among the team.

7.4 Neural Networks for Anomaly Detection in Microservices

Neural networks have turned out to be the foundation of present day anomaly detection in microservices, due to the ability to learn what has been considered normal in high dimensional and non-stationary settings and identify subtle deviations with no hand-crafted rules. Most anomalies in the distributed system do not occur as hard failures, but in changes in behavior—a service will continue to respond, but with new latency patterns, error mixes, or dependencies. Detectors of neural anomalies are therefore trained on normal data and consider significant deviations as possible incidents as opposed to using a fixed threshold.

In microservice environments, conspicuous labels of all types of anomalies are few, partial, or soon out of date. The failure modes are emerging with the evolution of architectures, even with the absence of such failure modes in the historical occurrence. This is why most neural methods use a paradigm of unsupervised or semi-unsupervised methods: they are only (or mostly) trained on the traces and measures and logs of normal functioning, and they learn a low-level internal description of normal functioning. During inference, the model does not provide answers to the question of which class this is, but rather the question of how far away is this to what I regard as normal.

The three basic properties of microservice environments addressed in this reframing are as follows:

- **Open-ended anomaly space:** There are no failure modes that can be listed beforehand.

- **Concept drift:** Different ideas of normalness change over time as services are redeployed, scaled, and refactored.
- **High dimensionality:** Each service generates a lot of metrics; when multiplied by dozens of services, naive rule sets get out of control.

Neural networks overcome these issues because they self-learn low-dimensional latent spaces that normal behavior occupies as high density regions. Likewise, anomalies are represented as outliers.

7.4.1 Autoencoders (AE): Learning Compact Representations

Autoencoders are feed-forward neural networks trained to relearn their input. They are divided into two major sections:

- **Encoder:** Reduces the input features (e.g., latency, error rate, CPU usage, memory consumption, queue lengths) into a reduced-dimensional latent feature.
- **Decoder:** Tries to recover the original input based on this compressed version.

The autoencoder is only trained to optimize the representation of usual patterns using normal data. It fails to faithfully reconstruct abnormal combinations of features that do not match its training distribution, giving it a high reconstruction error.

Typical workflow:

- **Inputs:** Aggregated metrics of a service or a small service group using windows.
- **Loss:** Loss function mean squared error (MSE) or other reconstruction loss between input and output.
- **Anomaly score:** The per-sample reconstruction error, where the value is substantially larger than the distribution of normalized reconstruction errors. This is counted as an anomaly.

The strategy can be used especially with the following:

- Identifying abrupt and multi-metric changes (e.g., latency and CPU burst occur in a pattern not observed during training).
- In environments where the relationships between metrics are more significant than the exact values.
- Cases when the sample of labeled anomalies is infrequent or invalid.

7.4.2 AE–LSTM Hybrids: Temporal Aware Reconstruction

The conventional autoencoders look at each input vector separately. The most common anomalies in microservices, though, are observed as time trends and not as instantaneous bursts, medium-scale memory consumption, gradual latency rise, or queue saturation. Hybrids AE LSTM hybrids build on the autoencoder concept, but in the time-series, with sequence modeling and reconstruction.

Typical AE–LSTM design:

- The encoder is implemented as one or more LSTM layers operating over sequences of metric vectors, compressing a time window into a latent representation that encodes both current state and recent history.
- The decoder is another LSTM (or sequence of dense layers) that reconstructs the original temporal sequence from the latent state.

This architecture excels at:

- Detecting gradual drifts (e.g., memory leakage), where each time step is nearly normal but the overall sequence is not typical.
- Capturing recurring daily or weekly rhythms and flagging behavior that breaks those rhythms.
- Differentiating between short-lived spikes (often benign) and consistent, pattern-breaking trends (often precursors to failure).

Since the hybrid is still trained with normal sequences, reconstruction error is used as the primary signal. However, error is no longer measured at time points, but at sequences. Deviations that would not be observed by snapshot-based systems are uncovered in the long term.

7.5 Graph Neural Networks (GNN): Topology-Aware Detection

Microservices rarely fail in isolation. Their behavior is shaped by network calls, retries, backpressure, and cascading timeouts across service boundaries. GNNs explicitly embed this topology into the detection process by treating:

- Nodes as services (or sometimes pods, endpoints, or even trace spans).
- Edges as API calls, message queues, or other communication relationships.

Features on nodes (e.g., service-level metrics) and edges (e.g., call latency, error rate) are passed through GNN layers, which aggregate and transform information from neighbors. This allows the model to learn patterns such as these:

- "Service A is healthy unless Services B and C are simultaneously degraded."
- "An anomaly originating in a single database service will propagate along certain edges but spare others."

GNN-based detectors are especially strong at:

- **Localized anomaly detection:** It will support the detection of the subgraphs (sets of services) with anomalous behavior and not the entire system.
- **Root-cause guidance:** It is possible to allocate the anomalies to likely source services instead of just specifying downstream manifestations because of the graphical representation of the model.
- **Handling topology changes:** When new and existing services are added and removed, an update to the graph can be made. In most cases, structural patterns can be learned in generalized form by the GNN.

Combining GNNs with time-varying models (such as LSTMs or attention mechanisms) creates architectures that can learn where and when anomalies exist, which is true in the complex reality of microservice deployments.

7.6 Foundation Guide Autoencoder Implementation

The following autoencoder pattern provides a solid starting point for metric-based anomaly detection at the service level. It assumes you are working with fixed-size feature vectors representing a snapshot or short window of metrics for a given service.

7.6.1 Model Definition and Training

```
from tensorflow.keras.layers import Input, Dense
from tensorflow.keras.models import Model

input_dim = X_train.shape[1]

input_layer = Input(shape=(input_dim,))
encoded = Dense(32, activation='relu')(input_layer)
decoded = Dense(input_dim, activation='sigmoid')(encoded)

autoencoder = Model(inputs=input_layer, outputs=decoded)
autoencoder.compile(optimizer='adam', loss='mse')

history = autoencoder.fit(
    X_train,
    X_train,
    epochs=50,
    batch_size=128,
    validation_split=0.1,
    shuffle=True,
    verbose=1
)
```

Key design points:

- **Input:** `X_train` must include only (or mostly only) samples in the normal operation of the system, once it has been suitably normalized (e.g. min-max scaling or standardization) so that all measures have a similar scale.

- **Bottleneck size (32 here):** Determines the force of the compression. Smaller values make the model follow only the most fundamental patterns and can tend to enhance the sensitivity to the anomaly, but excessive values can cause low reconstruction of even normal data.
- **Loss (MSE):** This is the closeness of the reconstructed outputs to the inputs; it can be applied to particular distributions.

7.6.2 Deriving the Anomaly Score

Once the training is done, you calculate reconstruction errors on a set of knowns of normal samples on a validation set and save the distribution. A common approach is as follows:

```
import numpy as np
reconstructions = autoencoder.predict(X_train)
train_errors = np.mean(np.square(X_train - reconstructions), axis=1)
mean_err = np.mean(train_errors)
std_err  = np.std(train_errors)
# Example static threshold at mean + 2σ
threshold = mean_err + 2 * std_err
```

For each new sample x at runtime:

1. Compute its reconstruction x̂.
2. Calculate the reconstruction error `e = MSE(x, x̂)`.
3. Flag x as anomalous if e > threshold (or feed e into downstream logic as a continuous anomaly score rather than a hard binary decision).

7.6.3 Operational Integration

In order to make this part of the operational observability stack in a microservice environment, follow these steps:

1. **Inference service**

    - Containerize the trained autoencoder as a lightweight service (e.g., in a Python/Flask or FastAPI container) that co-locates with your monitoring system or runs as a sidecar.

    - The service provides an endpoint where the metric vectors are accepted and a reconstruction error is returned (and sometimes the reconstructed metrics are provided to aid debugging).

2. **Prometheus metric export**

    - Estimate the reconstruction error service or instance in a periodic manner (e.g., every 30-60 seconds).

    - Expose a custom metric, for example:

      `service_reconstruction_error{service="checkout", instance="pod-123"}`

    - Prometheus scrapes these metrics via the standard `/metrics` endpoint.

3. **Alerting strategy**

    - Estimate alerting levels of history reconstruction error distributions. Commonly, an alarm is roused when the error exceeds `2sigma` or `3sigma` of the normal mean in the long term, and does not occur on a single sample peak.

    - Integrate anomaly signals with domain-constrained conditions (e.g., only alert on anomalies coexisting with user-observable latency degradation).

4. **Visualization and analysis**

    - Grafana dashboards show reconstruction error through time, it may be overlayed with major business KPIs.

    - The operators can see which services have increasing scores on the anomaly and match them with deployment or configuration changes or breaking dependencies.

7.6.4 Extending Toward AE–LSTM and GNN

Although the simple feed-forward autoencoder offers an easy point of entry, most production-level productions of anomaly detection of microservices develop along two dimensions:

- **Temporal extension:** Use LSTM layers instead of the dense encoder/decoder to transition snapshot-based anomaly scoring to sequence-aware detection. This provides the ability to detect slow drifts and pattern changes as time goes by.
- **Topological extension:** Model the microservice system as a graph and use a GNN (or graph-attention model) to enable anomalies to be distributed on services and dependency patterns instead of just being detected at a global metric scale.

By starting with the basic autoencoder and adding temporal and graph-sensitive functionality in increasing layers, groups can create a neural anomaly detector stack that can scale as complex as microservices do, but that can be explained and managed in existing monitoring and incident response processes.

7.7 Predictive Analytics for Resource and Performance Optimization

Most of the so-called faults are merely tardy symptoms of resource overloading, which can be anticipated when the CPU, memory, I/O, or connection pools are depleted. Time-series models are concerned with multiple regimes:

- **ARIMA/Prophet:** Best for linear trends and strong seasonality (e.g., daily traffic waves, weekly load cycles).
- **LSTM/GRU:** Capture multi-metric, nonlinear load patterns where CPU, latency, and queue depths interact.
- **Reinforcement learning (RL):** Learns policies that optimize resource allocation decisions (scale up/down, reroute traffic) based on reward signals such as SLO adherence and cost.

A typical closed-loop control looks like this: Forecast → Raise predictive alert → Kubernetes HPA (or custom scaler) adjusts replicas/resources → Observe resulting performance → Feed outcome back into the model and policy.

Foundation guide: Prophet forecasting (brief):

- Prophet uses historical information to predict the CPU and memory demand in the short-term.
- Visualize the predicted CPU_pred/mem_pred with your metrics pipeline and graph them alongside real usage on Grafana dashboards.
- Define examples of centrality. For example, if the anticipated CPU is larger than 80 percent over the next N intervals, scale beforehand and connect to auto-scaling or runbooks.

7.8 Prometheus and Grafana Monitoring and Visualization

The predictive and ML-based fault signals can be utilized only when they are visible, queryable, observable, and understandable by humans.

Prometheus strengths:

- Pull-based scraping simplifies the complexity of agents and centralizes the process of metrics gathering.
- Metric models with a lot of labels go hand in hand with microservices (service, instance, region, version, canary ring).
- PromQL can be used to perform temporal queries, percentiles (p90/p99 latency), and rate/derivative queries. Essential for SLOs.

Grafana strengths:

- Transforms raw series into dashboards, heatmaps, correlation panels, and anomaly overlays.
- Visualizes ML outputs (e.g., fault probability, forecast, reconstructions errors) with Prometheus, InfluxDB, or JSON/HTTP sources.
- Favors per-team (SRE, security, product) projections based on the same underlying metrics.

Guidebook foundation guide: Prometheus and Grafana setup:

- Have Prometheus scrape the `/metrics` endpoints of microservices on a short frequency (e.g., 15s); contain raw measures as well as ML calculated indicators (e.g., fault probability).
- Open Grafana and integrate it with Prometheus; create dashboards to superimpose:
- Measures of the present vs. expected results (CPU vs. CPU pred).

  Autoencoder anomaly scores vs. LSTM anomaly scores.

Route Prometheus notifies webhooks via Alert Manager or chat or remediation bots. These ML-driven alerts are brought under the same on-call workflow as their brethren.

7.9 Security-Aware Fault Prediction

Misconfiguration, dependency drift, and runtime abnormality tend to overlap as precursors to operation errors and security attacks. Making them separate also conceals valuable correlations.

Key correlations to exploit:

- **Fault-prone modules:** Increased concentration of vulnerable libraries and CVEs
- **High redeploy frequency:** Configuration and permission drift risk
- **Abnormal outbound traffic:** Possible data leakage or command and control

Pipeline integration patterns: block deployment if fault risk >0.7 AND critical CVE count>0 for internet-facing service

- Create SBOMs (e.g., through Syft) and perform vulnerability scans (e.g., through Trivy) on the CI/CD pipeline.
- Combine aggregate indicators, such as critical CVE count, the introduction of new vulnerable packages, and config change density into the same feature set as the fault-risk prediction.
- Specify combined risks policies (e.g., block deployment) or obtain further approvals when the forecasted fault risk and security exposure both cross certain thresholds.

Foundation guide for Trivy and Syft

- **Syft:** Generates SBOMs for each service (JSON or SPDX) and inputs package/version metadata into your ML feature store.
- **Trivy:** Scans the filesystem or images to compute the number of critical/high vulnerabilities; transmits the number and the severity distributions as model features.
- As time progresses, determines the strongest combinations of vulnerabilities and operational signals associated with incidents.

7.10 Monitoring and Visualization with Prometheus and Grafana

Predictive and ML-based fault signals are only useful when they are observable, queryable, and understandable by humans.

Prometheus strengths:

- Pull-based scraping reduces agent complexity and centralizes metric collection.
- Label-rich metric model aligns naturally with microservices (service, instance, region, version, canary ring).
- PromQL enables temporal queries, percentiles (p90/p99 latency), and rate/derivative calculations essential for SLOs.

Grafana strengths:

- Converts raw series into dashboards, heatmaps, correlation panels, and anomaly overlays.
- Can visualize ML outputs (e.g., fault probabilities, forecasts, reconstruction errors) using Prometheus, InfluxDB, or JSON/HTTP data sources.
- Supports per-team views (SRE, security, product) built over the same underlying metrics.

Foundation guide: Prometheus and Grafana setup (brief):

- Configure Prometheus to scrape microservices' `/metrics` endpoints on a short interval (e.g., 15s); include raw metrics and ML-derived signals (e.g., `fault_probability`).
- Run Grafana and connect it to Prometheus; build dashboards that overlay:
    - Current metrics vs. predicted metrics (CPU vs. CPU_pred)
    - Error rates vs. anomaly scores from autoencoders or LSTMs
- Route Prometheus alerts through Alert Manager to webhooks, chat, or remediation bots, so ML-driven alerts participate in the same on-call workflow as traditional ones.

7.11 Self-Healing Systems and AIOps

Self-healing architectures close the loop between observation, diagnosis, and action. They use AIOps techniques to correlate events, prioritize signals, and automate low-risk remediation.

The canonical pipeline is as follows: Metrics/logs/traces → ML-based anomaly detector → Diagnosis and correlation (AIOps) → Remediation engine (orchestrator, runbooks, bots) → Feedback loop to models and policies.

Core building blocks:

- AIOps platforms for event correlation, deduplication, and incident clustering; they turn a storm of alerts into a smaller set of actionable situations.
- RL or policy engines that learn which remediation actions (restart, rollback, scale, failover) are most effective in given contexts.
- Knowledge graphs capturing system topology and historical "symptom → root cause → fix" relationships.

Foundation guide: Kubernetes self-healing example (brief):

- Use liveness and readiness probes to automatically restart failing health checks of unhealthy pods in Kubernetes.
- Send anomaly notifications through push (Prometheus/Alert Manager) into a remediation controller or GitOps system (e.g. Argo CD) via webhooks.
- Use guarded automation. Should the action not be high stakes (scale restart), it can be automated. However it is high stakes (rollback across regions), it can be supervised by humans but pre-filled with advice.

7.12 Human-in-the-Loop and Explainable AI

With more automated fault prediction, operators need to know and review the reason behind the decision. Explainable AI (XAI) ensures that models do not blind people but rather enhance their judgment.

Key XAI tools and artifacts:

- **SHAP values:** Measures the contribution of each feature to a particular prediction (e.g., 80 percent of this alert was defined by a new dependency on critical CVEs and recent spikes in errors).
- **LIME:** Constructs local interpretable approximations around any single prediction, assisting the engineer in debugging model behavior on difficult cases.
- **Model cards:** Provides brief documentation of training data—what it is to be used, restrictions, and performance, which should comply with governance and compliance requirements.

Workflow example:

1. The model flags a deployment as high-risk.
2. According to XAI tools, the bulk of the risk signal is driven by a new unvetted dependency and a flakiest test of the module.
3. The engineer verifies the SBOM and recent configuration changes, accepts the issue, and selects rollback or further hardening.

There is still human responsibility in this trend: models are patterns and recommendations to humans, and engineers make the final decision, which is based on open logic.

7.13 Challenges and Research Frontiers

The practical realization of advanced fault prediction within microservice ecosystems is not merely a question of algorithms but of endurance models, infrastructure, and governance. The following sections examine the persistent obstacles that limit maturity today and the research avenues that will define the next generation of predictive, self-healing systems.

7.13.1 Data Drift and Continuous Retraining

Every predictive model gets out of step with reality over time. The data is distributed depending on the varying behavior of the users, patterns of traffic, and the infrastructure. A model will soon start mistyping edge cases and will not generalize new ways of failure. This is a silent sabotage of dependability such as gradual leaking of information of degeneration.

Nowadays, retraining is a direct component of DevSecOps teams. It is not fixed, but is a living process that is constantly being tested and renewed periodically. In GitHub Actions, GitLab CI, or Jenkins, drift-detecting tools such as Evidently AI can be applied and the predicted results can be compared to the observed ones. When the accuracy or recall decreases to a level that is below set limits, the pipeline is automatically re-trained on new production telemetry.

It is also important to have lineage tracking. MLflow and DVC have versioned histories in which data, code, and model weights are stored, enabling teams to rerun any training run or roll back when retraining a model makes it worse than its predecessor. Cloud orchestration frameworks such as AWS SageMaker Pipelines, Azure ML, and Vertex AI run retraining cycles with frequency—daily in volatile workloads, weekly in general SaaS systems, and monthly in stable industrial systems.

A particularly elegant example is the open-source project `evidentlyai/evidently`, which generates automatic performance dashboards and drift reports suitable for inclusion in CI workflows.

7.13.2 Federated Learning and Data Governance

Many organizations cannot centralize telemetry for regulatory or competitive reasons. Healthcare providers, banks, and multi-tenant cloud operators must retain data sovereignty while still benefiting from collective learning. Federated learning offers a balance.

In a federated system, each node—whether a cluster, region, or organization—trains a local model on its own data. Only the parameter updates are shared with the central aggregator, which merges them into a global model and redistributes the result. Raw data does not leave its source, so it does not compromise GDPR, HIPAA, and so on.

This approach is a viable one outside academia with the aid of open-source projects like TensorFlow Federated, Flower, and FedML. Flower enables developers to federate existing PyTorch and Keras models with only slight adjustments, and FedML federates edge environments and Kubernetes clusters.

Challenges remain. Federated training is negatively affected by the significantly uneven (non-IID) data of participants or the network latency that hinders synchronization. Current studies in adaptive learning rates, gradient compression, and Byzantine-resilient aggregation are still enhancing the scalability and robustness to enable reliable cross-organizational fault-prediction networks.

7.13.3 Edge Inference and Model Compression

Predictive intelligence has to spend most of the time inside the systems that it is protecting. Computational budgets in edge gateways, IoT controllers, or Kubernetes Sidecar are small and memory footprints are small. The aggressive optimization is required for deploying full-size deep models in such environments.

The most common techniques that prevail in this space are quantization and knowledge distillation. Quantization minimizes numerical accuracy. By converting 32-bit floating-point weights to 8-bit integers, models are reduced by up to 75 percent with little or no loss of accuracy. Distillation, in contrast, takes the knowledge of a big-teacher model and transfers it into a small-student by training it with soft-targets.

This is easily done using frameworks like TensorFlow Lite, PyTorch Quantization, and ONNX runtime, and Apache TVM is a compiler of optimized binaries, tailored to a particular CPU and accelerator. Together these tools allow models previously limited to GPU to run efficiently on container nodes or ARM-based gateways.

An actual workflow can make a 100MB LSTM anomaly detector a 6MB quantized student network that can be deployed to the edge with a trade-off in accuracy that is only slightly worse off than full-floating, intelligent fault prediction—something to show that intelligent fault prediction does not have to be resource intensive.

7.13.4 Securing the Machine-Learning Pipeline

The pipeline is an object as ML becomes part of the operational control. Attackers can either attempt to poison training data, modify stored models, or compromise inference endpoints to cause false remediation. The answer here is a zero-trust ML pipeline—a system in which each component authenticates the rest of the components before sharing data or taking any action.

Artifacts have to be cryptographically signed and verified. Sigstore Cosign is a graceful implementation, and it can be integrated into CI/CD systems to sign model tarballs or ONNX packages:

```
cosign sign --key cosign.key model.tar.gz
cosign verify model.tar.gz
```

The control should reach all the layers: role-scoped permissions in Kubeflow, granular RBAC permissions in orchestration levels, and short-lived just-in-time tokens in training jobs. Other auxiliary tools like Great Expectations check the consistency of incoming data to the schema and identify potential poisoning attempts, whereas MLflow keeps lineage metadata to trace any potentially compromised model on the inputs of its training process.

Together, these practices establish end-to-end integrity: every dataset, model, and inference call is authenticated, signed, and auditable.

7.13.5 Benchmarking and Open Datasets

The development of fault prediction has been accomplished at a quicker rate than benchmarks. Algorithms cannot be guesswork. Current base tools such as PMLB, OpenML, and Numenta Anomaly Benchmark (NAB) provide good baselines, but none of them models the multi-temporal, multi-service dynamics of modern microservice environments.

The gap is beginning to be bridged. Kubernetes Operational traces in anonymized format. AIOps Benchmark Consortium and labeled real-world metrics are offered by AWS. However, a publicly available, domain-specific microservice fault benchmark (MFB) data comes in the form of traces and SBOMs. The annotation of failures is an excellent necessity. Benchmarking must not only be accurate. Being able to identify problems in their early stages, latency impact, and root cause determination must all be accurate. By setting up such metrics, quick comparison, reproducibility, and adoption will be achieved in the end.

7.13.6 Agentic AI and Autonomous Security Operations

The final frontier merges predictive modeling with reasoning. Agentic AI systems extend today's reactive automation into goal-oriented decision-making. Rather than blindly scaling resources when latency rises, an agent analyzes telemetry, consults historical context, evaluates compliance constraints, and determines whether to scale, tune, or investigate. Table 7-1 shows AI Driven operational frameworks for monitoring, automation, and governance.

Table 7-1. *Category wise project example with function*

Category	Example Project	Function
Observability agents	grafana/agent and custom LLM hooks	Stream telemetry to AI models
AIOps framework	opsmx/enterprise-spinnaker	Policy-driven automated rollbacks
Agentic orchestration	LangChain and OpenDevin	Build reasoning agents for incident response
Security automation	StackStorm/st2	Event-driven SOAR platform integrating LLMs

Research prototypes and open-source projects are already beginning to adopt this paradigm. Reasoning agent frameworks like LangChain and OpenDevin can be used to build reasoning agents to communicate with observability data, and StackStorm and OpsMx Spinnaker incorporate these agents into continuous-delivery workflows. An observability agent written using Grafana Agent may, for example, send metrics to an LLM-based decision engine, which then writes pull requests or makes policy-verified rollbacks using Argo CD.

The concept of agentic AI raises new governance issues: how can one audit a decision made autonomously, how can one align agent goals with business intent, and how can one defend reasoning models against prompt or metric injection attacks? Guidelines like ISO 42001 and the AI Risk Management Framework created by NIST have become the standard, yet the work on the practical implementation is still an open research question.

The future research agenda entails explainable chains of reasoning, adversarial resilience, intent alignment, and coordination of multiple acting agents in the performance, cost, and security areas.

7.13.7 Concluding Perspective

High-level prediction of faults is moving toward adaptive intelligence as opposed to statistical foresight. The mentioned challenges include data drift, privacy-preserving learning, efficient edge inference, pipeline hardening, benchmarking, and agentic automation.

Practitioners must base experimentation on the following open-source ecosystems:

- **Evidently AI:** Drift detection and model monitoring
- **MLflow/DVC:** Reproducible model lifecycle management
- **Sigstore Cosign:** Artifact signing for secure deployment
- **TensorFlow Federated/Flower:** Privacy-preserving training
- **ONNX Runtime/TVM:** Portable and optimized inference
- **LangChain/StackStorm:** Foundations for autonomous operations

To continue reading, the Google SRE Book, *NISTs AI Risk Management Framework* (2023), and the *Flower Federated Learning* whitepaper (USENIX 2022) are thoroughly contextual. Combined, these sources describe a field that has begun to focus not on reactive maintenance, but on predictive, self-directed infrastructures (i.e., systems that not only identify and remedy their own failures, but also learn through every experience to make the next one better).

7.14 Conclusion

Advanced fault prediction has matured into a core DevSecOps competency.

- Machine learning provides statistical foresight.
- Deep learning captures complex system dynamics.
- Security integration ties fault risk to vulnerability posture.
- Prometheus and Grafana provide real-time situational awareness.
- AIOps and self-healing architectures close the loop with autonomous remediation.

DevSecOps can be changed into adaptive resilience engineering by combining predictive analytics with secure automation; this transforms reactive defense into proactive resilience engineering. Chapter 8 switches to the topic of implementation design to deploy such predictive systems into actual CI/CD pipelines and validate models on a regular basis, thus providing governance alignment.

CHAPTER 8

Building a Fault Prediction Framework in Microservice Architectures

Building a fault-forecasting model of any microservice architecture requires a methodical approach that will not only handle the complexity of distributed systems but also react to the existing DevSecOp's attitude on security. In comparison to the monolithic systems, where fault detection is reasonably local, microservices introduce fault domains that cross service boundaries, service layers of orchestration, and deployment lines. In order to make predictive decisions in these environments, a combined structure is required that can correlate operational telemetry to deployment metadata with security posture to make actionable predictions.

This chapter discusses the architectural ideas, information clauses, and verification processes used in the application of fault-prediction systems in microservice-based systems. It is concerned with the security-first observability model, which is no longer restricted to performance metrics but also vulnerability intelligence, runtime anomalies, and compliance factors. The seven stages included in the process of transforming raw metrics to production forecasts are defining organizational requirements, choice of metrics and datasets, model training, integration of build-time security, pre-deployment security evaluation, runtime verification, and ongoing validation. Each phase has an operational connection that creates a feedback mechanism, which adds value to the framework over time.

D. Sharma and A. Syed, *Fault Detection in Microservice Architectures*,
https://doi.org/10.1007/979-8-8688-2712-9_8

8.1 Defining Organizational Requirements for Distributed Fault Prediction

Predicting faults in a distributed ecosystem must commence with expressed organizational and architectural requirements. Unlike monolithic systems, microservices run in a complex dependency graph, changing executing environments and no-trust boundaries. In this respect, the technical constraints must be included in the requirements along with the security governance policies.

8.1.1 Microservice-Specific Requirements

1. **Cascading failure prevention**

   The models of service dependency are likely to take into account the interdependence of services to determine the emergence of cascading faults. As an example, an authentication service in an upstream spike can be a bottleneck in other supporting APIs. The propagation paths must be modeled within the framework in order to prioritize risk mitigation.

2. **Service dependency mapping**

   Synchronous and asynchronous communication patterns need to be tracked. The fault prediction should possess accurate dependency maps, that is, REST APIs, message queues, and external services. The predictive model can also be enhanced by automated generating graphs using service mesh telemetry (e.g., Istio, Linkerd) in order to capture real patterns of communication, rather than architecture diagrams.

3. **Partial failure handling**

   In distributed systems, failure of components in isolation is common. The structure should differentiate localized degradation and systemic instability, with the aid of graceful degradation policies and fallback mechanisms (e.g., circuit breakers, bulkheads). The system of fault prediction that considers all failures as equal will raise too many false alarms, and this will undermine the confidence of the team.

4. **Stateless service considerations**

   A significant portion of microservices are stateless (i.e., conventional persistence-based indicators of failure) and are not applicable. The prediction framework must concern itself with short-lived runtime indicators, including container health, response latency, and service mesh telemetry.

8.1.2 Security and Compliance Integration

The issue of security does not coincide with the second layer in fault prediction. The principles of DevSecOps need to be instituted initially:

- Container image scanning should not be done after the ingestion of the metrics to the prediction system. Having a vulnerable base image can lead to a runtime vulnerability and an exploitable vulnerability. A service using a container with an unpatched critical vulnerability is potentially vulnerable and exploitable.
- Access to service credentials and configuration secrets should be managed by the prediction frameworks. Integration to solutions based on vaults (e.g., HashiCorp Vault, AWS Secrets Manager) is necessary to make prediction agents work without revealing sensitive data.
- Auditable events, such as fault predictions, which provoke the rollback of deployments should be logged. In controlled contexts (e.g., PCI DSS, HIPAA), it is essential to have a trace of the decisions made during fault prediction and the deployment activities.
- The framework should treat all service-to-service communication as untrusted until verified. This ensures that prediction pipelines cannot be spoofed or tampered with by compromised components.

8.1.3 Scalability and Multi-Tenancy Requirements

The system of microservices can be distributed into various clusters, regions, and clouds. An industrial quality prediction system has to:

- Scale horizontally to analyze thousands of microservice instances concurrently.
- Support multi-cluster contexts, enabling cross-cluster correlation between metrics and deployment data.
- Operate with low latency, ensuring predictions can influence autoscaling and rollout decisions in near real-time.
- Optimize computational cost, using sampling, caching, and model compression techniques to prevent prediction systems from becoming cost-prohibitive.

8.2 Selecting Metrics and Training Datasets for Microservice Environments

8.2.1 Phase 1: Data Collection Infrastructure

The first step before choosing metrics is to establish the basis of observability on which your prediction models will run.

Prometheus for Metrics Collection

Configure Prometheus scrape targets for each microservice using `/metrics` endpoints with a scrape interval of 15-30 seconds. Set up a Kubernetes service discovery to automatically detect new services. Configure metric retention for at least 30 days to support training data collection.

```
# prometheus.yml configuration
global:
  scrape_interval: 30s
  evaluation_interval: 30s
```

```
scrape_configs:
  - job_name: 'microservices'
    kubernetes_sd_configs:
      - role: pod
    metric_relabel_configs:
      - source_labels: [__name__]
        regex: '(http_requests_total|http_request_duration_seconds|process_
        resident_memory_bytes|container_cpu_usage_seconds_total)'
        action: keep
```

APM and Distributed Tracing

Install APM agents (New Relic, Dynatrace, Datadog) to obtain end-to-end service traces. Calculate percentiles (P50, P95, P99) of the latency of each service endpoint. Trace service-to-service call trails and dependency chains. Gather transaction error rates and trace completion rates; these provide contextual information regarding service health other than raw counts of requests.

Kubernetes Events and Audit Logs

Enabling the Kubernetes audit logging will help monitor the pod scheduling, eviction, and state changes. Collect deployment metadata like image versions, replica, configuration count, node pressure failure, resource constraint violation, and restart of track pods. These incidences provide a history of framework pressure, which is a prelude to faults on the application level.

8.2.2 Phase 2: Defining and Labeling Faults

Create precise fault definitions to generate reliable training labels. Rather than detecting individual bugs, define faults as:

- Service failures (pod not running for >60 seconds)
- SLA violations (response latency exceeds p99 threshold by >30 percent)
- Error rate spikes (5xx errors exceed 5 percent of traffic for >2 minutes)

- Resource exhaustions (CPU/memory saturation causing pod eviction)
- Cascading failures (service degradation detected within five minutes of dependent service failure)

The training label should be a 30-minute pre-incident window. This guarantees that the model will acquire precursor patterns and not post-failure artifacts. A service that exhibits high latency and high error rates 20 minutes prior to a total outage is the best training signal and is early enough to allow preventive measures, yet associated enough to be causal.

```
# Pseudocode for fault labeling
def label_fault_windows(metrics_df, incidents_df):
    """
    Create binary fault labels for training data

    Args:
        metrics_df: Time-series metrics (timestamp, service, metric_value)
        incidents_df: Historical incidents (start_time, end_time, service,
        root_cause)

    Returns:
        Labeled dataset with fault_probability column
    """
    labeled_data = metrics_df.copy()
    labeled_data['fault'] = 0

    for _, incident in incidents_df.iterrows():
        # Create 30-minute pre-incident window as "high risk"
        fault_window = (
            (labeled_data['timestamp'] >= incident['start_time'] -
            pd.Timedelta(minutes=30)) &
            (labeled_data['timestamp'] <= incident['end_time']) &
            (labeled_data['service'] == incident['service'])
        )
        labeled_data.loc[fault_window, 'fault'] = 1

    return labeled_data
```

8.2.3 Phase 3: Handling Class Imbalance

In microservice systems, faulty states are less common than healthy states (usually 99:1 or worse). The naive models will assume that everything is healthy and overlook critical failures.

The most effective strategy in high-dimensional data (100 or more features, based on complex topologies of services) is stratified K-fold cross-validation with SMOTE:

1. Separate healthy and faulty samples.
2. Apply stratified undersampling for the healthy class, reducing the faulty sample count five times.
3. Use SMOTE during cross-validation (fit on training fold only) to generate synthetic minority samples.
4. Create a pipeline ensuring that SMOTE is applied post-split to prevent data leakage.

This approach reduces computational cost, prevents data leakage between train/test splits, and maintains fault class distribution in each fold.

Stratified K-Fold with Undersampling

```
from imblearn.over_sampling import SMOTE
from imblearn.pipeline import Pipeline
from sklearn.preprocessing import StandardScaler
from sklearn.model_selection import StratifiedKFold

# Step 1: Separate healthy and faulty samples
healthy = data[data['fault'] == 0]
faulty = data[data['fault'] == 1]

# Step 2: Apply stratified undersampling for healthy class
# Reduce healthy samples to 5x faulty sample count (1:5 ratio)
healthy_undersampled = healthy.sample(n=len(faulty) * 5, random_state=42)
balanced_data = pd.concat([healthy_undersampled, faulty])

# Step 3: Use SMOTE during cross-validation (fit on training fold only)
smote = SMOTE(sampling_strategy=0.5, random_state=42)  # 1:2 ratio
kfold = StratifiedKFold(n_splits=10, shuffle=True, random_state=42)
```

```
# Step 4: Create pipeline ensuring SMOTE applied post-split
pipeline = Pipeline([
    ('smote', SMOTE(sampling_strategy=0.5)),
    ('scaler', StandardScaler()),
    ('classifier', RandomForestClassifier(n_estimators=100))
])
```

Why this works better:

- Undersampling results in a lower computational cost (SMOTE is costly with high-dimensional data).
- SMOTE per-fold metrics eliminate leakage among train/test breaks.
- Stratified folds preserve distributions of the classes of faults in a split.
- The artificial examples formed in the course of training do not affect test performance.

8.2.4 Phase 4: Temporal Alignment

Microservice metrics are time-series in nature; set them up right to avoid model degradation. Resample the sparse service measures to a regular frequency (e.g., one-minute intervals). Add time-lagged features to capture time-variations. Add lagged values of the main metrics used such as latency, error rate, and memory used at time-delays of 5, 10, and 20 minutes.

Ensure that there is no leakage of future information into training features. Then confirm the absence of missing values, confirm the correctness of metric units and ranges, and eliminate outliers that indicate measurement errors and not faults.

```
# Ensure all service metrics align to same time intervals
def align_metrics_to_frequency(raw_metrics, target_frequency='1min'):
    """
    Resample sparse service metrics to consistent frequency

    Args:
        raw_metrics: DataFrame with irregular timestamps
        target_frequency: Target resampling frequency (e.g., '1min', '30s')

    Returns:
```

```
        Aligned metrics with forward-fill for missing data
    """
    aligned = raw_metrics.set_index('timestamp')
    aligned = aligned.resample(target_frequency).agg({
        'http_requests_total': 'sum',
        'http_request_duration_seconds': 'mean',
        'memory_bytes': 'last',
        'cpu_usage': 'mean'
    }).fillna(method='ffill')  # Forward fill for sparse metrics

    return aligned.reset_index()

# Create time-lagged features for each service
def create_lagged_features(metrics_df, lags=[5, 10, 20]):
    """
    Generate time-lagged features to capture temporal patterns

    Args:
        metrics_df: Aligned metrics
        lags: List of lag periods in minutes

    Returns:
        Features with lagged values for model training
    """
    for lag in lags:
        metrics_df[f'latency_p95_lag{lag}'] = metrics_df['latency_p95'].
        shift(lag)
        metrics_df[f'error_rate_lag{lag}'] = metrics_df['error_rate'].
        shift(lag)
        metrics_df[f'memory_usage_lag{lag}'] = metrics_df['memory_bytes'].
        shift(lag)

    # Drop rows with NaN from lag creation
    return metrics_df.dropna()
```

8.3 Microservice-Specific Metrics Selection

8.3.1 Health and Availability Metrics

The metrics outlined in Table 8-1 provide the strongest early indicators of service degradation.

Table 8-1. *Health and Availability Metrics*

Metric	Collection Method	Interpretation	Fault Indicator
Liveness probe status	Kubernetes HTTP GET to /health/live	Container is running and responsive	Persistent DOWN status predicts imminent pod restart or eviction
Readiness probe status	Kubernetes HTTP GET to /health/ready	Service ready to serve traffic	NOT_READY for >5 minutes indicates dependency issues or resource starvation
HTTP response latency (P95)	APM/Prometheus histogram	Request processing time at 95th percentile	2-3x increase often precedes error rate spikes within ten minutes
Error rate (5xx %)	`http_requests_total{status=~"5.."} / http_requests_total`	Proportion of server errors	Sudden spike (>5 percent sustained) is a high-confidence fault indicator
Request throughput (RPS)	`rate(http_requests_total[1m])`	Requests per second	Anomalous drops indicate load balancer issues or cascading failure

```
# Prometheus metrics configuration for health checks
apiVersion: v1
kind: Pod
metadata:
  name: microservice
spec:
  containers:
  - name: app
    image: myapp:latest
```

```
ports:
- name: metrics
  containerPort: 8080
livenessProbe:
  httpGet:
    path: /health/live
    port: 8080
  initialDelaySeconds: 30
  periodSeconds: 10
readinessProbe:
  httpGet:
    path: /health/ready
    port: 8080
  initialDelaySeconds: 5
  periodSeconds: 5
```

8.3.2 Resource Utilization Metrics

Capacity exhaustion is a leading cause of cascading failures:

- **Memory usage percent:** >90 percent sustained indicates OOM was killed likely within five minutes.
- **CPU usage percent:** >85 percent sustained causes throttling and latency spikes.
- **Database connection pool utilization:** >80 percent predicts connection timeouts.
- **Disk I/O utilization:** Sudden spikes correlate with database lock contentions.
- **Network interface saturation:** >70 percent indicates packet loss possibility.

8.3.3 Distributed System Metrics

Capture inter-service dependencies and cascading failure risks:

- **Inter-service call latency:** P95 latency from service A to B; >3x normal indicates downstream degradation.
- **Circuit breaker trip rate:** >0 trips/min indicates dependency service failing.
- **Retry rate:** >10 percent sustained indicates transient errors becoming persistent faults.
- **Service dependency error rate:** Sudden spike predicts cascading failure.

8.3.4 Container and Security Metrics

Runtime security anomalies correlate with security incidents and system instability:

- **CVE count in running images:** Increasing CVEs in production mean higher exploitation/instability risk.
- **Privilege escalation events:** Unexpected privilege escalations indicate compromise or misconfigurations.
- **Abnormal process execution:** Shells spawned in a container indicate potential compromises.
- **Resource limit violations:** Pod eviction is imminent when exceeding limits.

8.4 Model Training and Validation

8.4.1 Base Model Selection and Training

Begin with models that are interpretable and then investigate intricate ensembles. Random Forest is quick at offering a solid baseline, can interact with features, and offers feature importance. Gradient Boosting (GBM/LightGBM) has better accuracy and comes with built-in cross-validation. Neural networks are only to be used in the case of complex temporal dependence at the expense of interpretability.

Apply stratified ten-fold cross-validation on the balanced dataset. Precision in tracks, recall, F1 Score, AUC-ROC in all folds. Target performance measures must be as follows: Precision >0.75 (minimize false alarms), Recall >0.80 (detect real faults), F1 Score >0.75 (balanced measure), and AUC-ROC >0.85 (discrimination ability).

Here is the implementation:

```
from sklearn.ensemble import RandomForestClassifier,
GradientBoostingClassifier
from sklearn.model_selection import StratifiedKFold, cross_validate
from sklearn.metrics import precision_recall_curve, f1_score, roc_auc_score
import numpy as np
# Prepare training data
X = balanced_data.drop(['fault', 'timestamp', 'service'], axis=1)
y = balanced_data['fault']
# Step 1: Train Random Forest baseline
rf_model = RandomForestClassifier(
    n_estimators=100,
    max_depth=15,
    min_samples_split=10,
    class_weight='balanced',  # Weight minority class heavier
    n_jobs=-1,
    random_state=42
)
# Step 2: Cross-validation with stratified splits
kfold = StratifiedKFold(n_splits=10, shuffle=True, random_state=42)
cv_results = cross_validate(
    rf_model,
    X, y,
    cv=kfold,
    scoring=['precision', 'recall', 'f1', 'roc_auc'],
    return_train_score=True
)
```

```
# Step 3: Evaluate performance
print(f"Mean Precision: {cv_results['test_precision'].mean():.3f} (+/- {cv_
results['test_precision'].std():.3f})")
print(f"Mean Recall: {cv_results['test_recall'].mean():.3f} (+/- {cv_
results['test_recall'].std():.3f})")
print(f"Mean F1-Score: {cv_results['test_f1'].mean():.3f} (+/- {cv_
results['test_f1'].std():.3f})")
print(f"Mean AUC-ROC: {cv_results['test_roc_auc'].mean():.3f} (+/- {cv_
results['test_roc_auc'].std():.3f})")
```

8.4.2 Time-Series Cross-Validation

Standard cross-validation breaks temporal ordering; use expanding windows to simulate real deployment. Train on weeks 1–10; validate on week 11; train on weeks 1–11; validate on week 12. This approach avoids "future leakage" and mirrors real-world deployment progression.

```
def time_series_cross_validation(data, model, n_splits=5):
    """
    Implement expanding window cross-validation respecting time ordering

    Args:
        data: DataFrame with 'timestamp' and 'fault' columns
        model: Scikit-learn estimator
        n_splits: Number of CV splits

    Returns:
        Dictionary with per-fold metrics
    """
    data = data.sort_values('timestamp').reset_index(drop=True)
    n_samples = len(data)
    fold_size = n_samples // n_splits

    results = {'precision': [], 'recall': [], 'f1': [], 'auc_roc': []}

    for fold in range(n_splits):
        # Expanding window: train on weeks 1-N, validate on week N+1
```

```
        train_end = fold_size * (fold + 1)
        val_end = min(train_end + fold_size, n_samples)

        X_train = data.iloc[:train_end].drop(['fault',
        'timestamp'], axis=1)
        y_train = data.iloc[:train_end]['fault']

        X_val = data.iloc[train_end:val_end].drop(['fault',
        'timestamp'], axis=1)
        y_val = data.iloc[train_end:val_end]['fault']

        # Train and evaluate
        model.fit(X_train, y_train)
        y_pred = model.predict(X_val)
        y_proba = model.predict_proba(X_val)[:, 1]

        # Store metrics
        results['precision'].append(precision_score(y_val, y_pred))
        results['recall'].append(recall_score(y_val, y_pred))
        results['f1'].append(f1_score(y_val, y_pred))
        results['auc_roc'].append(roc_auc_score(y_val, y_proba))

    return results
```

8.4.3 Threshold Optimization

Different deployment contexts require different precision-recall tradeoffs. Generate precision-recall curves and select thresholds based on operational requirements. For fault prediction, prioritize recall (catch faults) over precision. Maximize the F1 Score for balanced performance, or target specific recall levels (e.g., 80% recall means you catch 80 percent of faults). See Table 8-2.

```
from sklearn.metrics import precision_recall_curve
# Train final model on full training set
model.fit(X, y)
# Generate predictions and probabilities
y_proba = model.predict_proba(X)[:, 1]
# Generate precision-recall curve
```

```
precision, recall, thresholds = precision_recall_curve(y, y_proba)
# Select threshold based on operational requirements
# For fault prediction: prioritize recall (catch faults) over precision
# Option 1: Maximize F1-score (balanced)
f1_scores = 2 * (precision[:-1] * recall[:-1]) / (precision[:-1] +
recall[:-1] + 1e-10)
optimal_idx = np.argmax(f1_scores)
optimal_threshold = thresholds[optimal_idx]
# Option 2: Target specific recall level (e.g., 80% recall = catch 80%
of faults)
target_recall_idx = np.argmin(np.abs(recall - 0.80))
conservative_threshold = thresholds[target_recall_idx]
print(f"Optimal threshold (F1 max): {optimal_threshold:.3f}")
print(f"Conservative threshold (80% recall): {conservative_threshold:.3f}")
```

Table 8-2. *Performance Metrics Interpretation*

Metric	Definition	Target	Rationale for Fault Prediction
Precision	TP / (TP + FP)	>0.75	Minimize false alarms; teams will ignore frequent false positives
Recall	TP / (TP + FN)	>0.80	Catch actual faults; missing real faults undermine the framework
F1 Score	2 × (Precision × Recall) / (Precision + Recall)	>0.75	Balanced metric for imbalanced fault datasets
AUC-ROC	Area under ROC curve	>0.85	Classifier discrimination capability across thresholds

8.5 Build-Time Integration: Container Security Scanning

8.5.1 Trivy Image Scanning in CI/CD

Prediction models are fed with metrics, which are scanned as container images. Add Trivy scanning to GitHub actions by following these steps:

1. Build a Docker image with a tagged SHA.
2. Run the Trivy image scan using the SARIF output format.
3. Parse the results and fail the build if critical vulnerabilities exceed thresholds.
4. Generate a software bill of materials (SBOM) in CycloneDX format.
5. Push the image to the registry only after passing the security scan.

```
# GitHub Actions workflow for container security
name: Container Image Security Scan
on: [push, pull_request]

jobs:
  build-and-scan:
    runs-on: ubuntu-latest
    steps:
      - uses: actions/checkout@v4

      - name: Build Docker Image
        run: |
          docker build -t myapp:${{ github.sha }} .
          docker tag myapp:${{ github.sha }} myapp:latest

      - name: Run Trivy Image Scan
        uses: aquasecurity/trivy-action@master
        with:
          image-ref: myapp:${{ github.sha }}
          format: 'sarif'
          output: 'trivy-results.sarif'
          severity: 'CRITICAL,HIGH'

      - name: Parse Trivy Results
        run: |
          CRITICAL_COUNT=$(jq '[.runs[0].results[] | select(.ruleId ==
          "CRITICAL")] | length' trivy-results.sarif)
          if [ "$CRITICAL_COUNT" -gt 0 ]; then
```

```
          echo "Found $CRITICAL_COUNT CRITICAL vulnerabilities"
          exit 1
        fi
        echo "Image passed security scan"

    - name: Generate SBOM
      run: |
        docker run --rm -v /var/run/docker.sock:/var/run/docker.sock \
          aquasec/trivy:latest image --format cyclonedx \
          --output sbom.json myapp:${{ github.sha }}

    - name: Push to Registry
      run: |
        docker push myapp:${{ github.sha }}
```

This ensures unsafe images never reach environments monitored by the fault-prediction system. Generate SBOMs and vulnerability evidence (VEX) for supply chain visibility.

8.5.2 Security Features for Prediction

Extract security metrics from container SBOMs to feed into your fault-prediction models:

- CVE count by severity (CRITICAL, HIGH, MEDIUM)
- Base image age in days
- Vulnerability remediation status

```
def extract_security_features(trivy_sbom, image_sha):
    """
    Extract security metrics from container SBOM for fault prediction

    Args:
        trivy_sbom: Trivy-generated SBOM JSON
        image_sha: Container image SHA for tracking

    Returns:
        Dictionary of security features for model input
    """
```

```
security_features = {
    'image_sha': image_sha,
    'cve_count_critical': 0,
    'cve_count_high': 0,
    'cve_count_medium': 0,
    'base_image_age_days': 0,
    'vuln_remediation_pending': False
}

# Extract vulnerability counts
for component in trivy_sbom.get('components', []):
    for vuln in component.get('vulnerabilities', []):
        severity = vuln.get('ratings', [{}])[0].get('severity',
        'UNKNOWN')
        if severity == 'CRITICAL':
            security_features['cve_count_critical'] += 1
        elif severity == 'HIGH':
            security_features['cve_count_high'] += 1
        elif severity == 'MEDIUM':
            security_features['cve_count_medium'] += 1

return security_features
```

These security metrics become features in your prediction models. A service that has been started containing containers with high-severity CVEs accumulating over time will exhibit a high probability of fault regardless of the latest performance indicators.

8.6 Pre-Deployment Risk Assessment and Intelligent Rollout

8.6.1 Calculating Deployment Risk Scores

Before deploying, combine code metrics, historical fault data, and prediction model output to generate deployment risk scores. Feature extraction for prediction includes:

- Error rate trends over the last 30 minutes
- Latency P95 trends

- Maximum CPU and memory utilization
- Circuit breaker trip count
- CVE count in new images
- Pod restart count in the last six hours

```
def calculate_deployment_risk(service_name, new_image_sha, historical_
metrics_df):
    """
    Generate deployment risk score for canary/rollout decisions

    Args:
        service_name: Name of microservice being deployed
        new_image_sha: Docker image SHA
        historical_metrics_df: Recent metrics for the service

    Returns:
        Risk score (0-100) and recommended deployment strategy
    """
    # Extract recent metrics (last 30 minutes)
    recent_metrics = historical_metrics_df[
        historical_metrics_df['timestamp'] >= pd.Timestamp.now() -
        pd.Timedelta(minutes=30)
    ]

    # Feature extraction for prediction
    features = {
        'error_rate_trend': recent_metrics['error_rate'].pct_
        change().mean(),
        'latency_p95_trend': recent_metrics['latency_p95'].pct_
        change().mean(),
        'memory_util_max': recent_metrics['memory_percent'].max(),
        'cpu_util_max': recent_metrics['cpu_percent'].max(),
        'circuit_breaker_trip_count': recent_metrics['cb_trips'].sum(),
        'cve_count_high': get_image_vuln_count(new_image_sha,
        severity='HIGH'),
        'recent_restarts': get_pod_restart_count(service_name, hours=6)
    }
```

```
# Run through trained prediction model
X = pd.DataFrame([features])
fault_probability = trained_model.predict_proba(X)[0, 1]

# Translate probability to deployment strategy
risk_score = fault_probability * 100

if risk_score < 5:
    strategy = 'FULL_ROLLOUT'
    description = 'Low risk, proceed with immediate full deployment'
elif risk_score < 15:
    strategy = 'CANARY_10PCT'
    description = '10% canary for 30min, monitor before full rollout'
elif risk_score < 30:
    strategy = 'CANARY_5PCT'
    description = '5% canary for 60min, staged rollout'
else:
    strategy = 'BLOCKED'
    description = 'High risk detected, manual review required'

return {
    'risk_score': risk_score,
    'strategy': strategy,
    'description': description,
    'contributing_factors': features
}
```

Run these features through your trained prediction model to generate a fault probability. Translate probability to your deployment strategy:

- **Risk score < 5 percent:** `FULL_ROLLOUT`—low risk, proceed with immediate full deployment.
- **Risk score 5-15 percent:** `CANARY_10PCT`—10 percent canary for 30 minutes, monitor before full rollout.
- **Risk score 15-30 percent:** `CANARY_5PCT`—5 percent canary for 60 minutes, staged rollout.
- **Risk score > 30 percent:** `BLOCKED`—high risk detected, manual review required.

8.6.2 Risk-Based Deployment Integration

Automatically compute risk scores into your pipeline. Output the score of the parsing risk, set the strategy of deployment according to the thresholds, and execute deployment according to the strategy. Apply a full rollout if you have low risk deployments. To use in medium risk deployments, trigger canary deployment with traffic splitting. For high-risk deployments, require manual approval or block deployment entirely.

```
# Deployment decision logic in GitHub Actions
- name: Assess Deployment Risk
  id: risk_assessment
  run: |
    RISK_SCORE=$(python risk_calculator.py --service myapp --image ${{
    github.sha }})
    echo "risk_score=$RISK_SCORE" >> $GITHUB_OUTPUT

    if (( $(echo "$RISK_SCORE < 5" | bc -l) )); then
      echo "strategy=FULL_ROLLOUT" >> $GITHUB_OUTPUT
    elif (( $(echo "$RISK_SCORE < 15" | bc -l) )); then
      echo "strategy=CANARY_10" >> $GITHUB_OUTPUT
    else
      echo "strategy=MANUAL_REVIEW" >> $GITHUB_OUTPUT
    fi

- name: Deploy with Strategy
  run: |
    if [ "${{ steps.risk_assessment.outputs.strategy }}" = "FULL_
    ROLLOUT" ]; then
      helm upgrade myapp ./chart --set image.tag=${{ github.sha }} --wait
    elif [ "${{ steps.risk_assessment.outputs.strategy }}" =
"CANARY_10" ]; then
      helm upgrade myapp ./chart --set canary.enabled=true --set canary.
      weight=10 --wait
    else
      echo "Deployment blocked for manual review"
      exit 1
    fi
```

8.7 Runtime Integration and Continuous Health Monitoring

8.7.1 Embedding Health Checks and Runtime Metrics

Configure Kubernetes pods with liveness and readiness probes feeding into the prediction system. Liveness probes detect dead containers; readiness probes detect dependency issues. Configure resource requests and limits to establish baseline capacity expectations.

```
apiVersion: apps/v1
kind: Deployment
metadata:
  name: microservice
spec:
  replicas: 3
  template:
    spec:
      containers:
      - name: app
        image: myapp:latest
        ports:
        - name: metrics
          containerPort: 8080

        # Health checks for pod lifecycle
        livenessProbe:
          httpGet:
            path: /health/live
            port: 8080
          initialDelaySeconds: 30
          periodSeconds: 10
          failureThreshold: 3

        readinessProbe:
          httpGet:
            path: /health/ready
```

```
            port: 8080
          initialDelaySeconds: 5
          periodSeconds: 5
          failureThreshold: 2

        # Resource requests/limits
        resources:
          requests:
            cpu: 100m
            memory: 256Mi
          limits:
            cpu: 500m
            memory: 512Mi

# Horizontal Pod Autoscaler with fault prediction integration
apiVersion: autoscaling/v2
kind: HorizontalPodAutoscaler
metadata:
  name: fault-prediction-hpa
spec:
  scaleTargetRef:
    apiVersion: apps/v1
    kind: Deployment
    name: microservice
  minReplicas: 2
  maxReplicas: 10
  metrics:
  - type: Resource
    resource:
      name: cpu
      target:
        type: Utilization
        averageUtilization: 70
  - type: Resource
    resource:
      name: memory
```

```
      target:
        type: Utilization
        averageUtilization: 80
  # Custom metric: fault probability
  - type: Pods
    pods:
      metric:
        name: fault_prediction_probability
      target:
        type: AverageValue
        averageValue: "0.5"  # Scale up if avg fault prob > 50%
```

8.7.2 Deploying Prediction Models as Microservices

Platforms such as KServe and Seldon Core support scalable and reliable model deployment in cloud-native environments. To improve service resilience, the serving layer should incorporate redundancy, load balancing, timeout controls, and fallback pathways. During temporary model outages, cached outputs, backup models, or rule-based logic can sustain critical operations, while automated recovery and graceful degradation help ensure uninterrupted pipeline performance. Scalable models use KServe or Seldon Core. Deploy predictive models by:

- Scheduling resources (CPU, memory) correctly
- Using inference load-based autoscaling
- Using canary deployments and model versioning
- Not changing the storage of model artifacts

```
apiVersion: serving.kserve.io/v1beta1
kind: InferenceService
metadata:
  name: fault-prediction-model
spec:
  predictor:
    model:
```

```
      modelFormat:
        name: sklearn
      storageUri: s3://ml-models/fault-predictor/v1
      resources:
        requests:
          cpu: 500m
          memory: 1Gi
        limits:
          cpu: 2
          memory: 4Gi
  autoscaler:
    minReplicas: 2
    maxReplicas: 10
    target: 80
    targetUtilizationPercentage: 80
```

8.7.3 Real-Time Prediction Pipeline

Implement a continuous prediction service that:

1. Queries Prometheus for recent service metrics every 30-60 seconds.
2. Formats metrics for model input.
3. Generates fault probability predictions.
4. Updates Prometheus metrics.
5. Stores results in Elasticsearch with metadata.

```
"""
Non-stop fault forecast service Kubernetes.
Reads Prometheus data, makes forecasts, writes to Elasticsearch.
"""

import requests
import json
from datetime import datetime, timedelta
```

```
import joblib
from prometheus_client import CollectorRegistry, Gauge

class FaultPredictionEngine:
    def __init__(self, model_path, prometheus_url, elasticsearch_host):
        self.model = joblib.load(model_path)
        self.prometheus_url = prometheus_url
        self.es_host = elasticsearch_host
        self.prediction_gauge = Gauge('fault_prediction_probability',
                                      'Fault prediction probability',
                                      ['service'])

    def fetch_service_metrics(self, service_name, lookback_minutes=30):
        """Query Prometheus for recent service metrics"""
        queries = {
            'error_rate': f'rate(http_requests_total{{service="{service_
            name}", status=~"5.."}}[5m])',
            'latency_p95': f'histogram_quantile(0.95, http_request_
            duration_seconds_bucket{{service="{service_name}"}})',
            'memory_percent': f'(container_memory_usage_bytes{{pod_
            label_app="{service_name}"}} / container_spec_memory_limit_
            bytes) * 100',
            'cpu_percent': f'rate(container_cpu_usage_seconds_total{{pod_
            label_app="{service_name}"}}[1m]) * 100',
        }

        metrics = {}
        for metric_name, query in queries.items():
            try:
                response = requests.get(f'{self.prometheus_url}/api/v1/
                query', params={'query': query})
                if response.status_code == 200:
                    result = response.json()['data']['result']
                    metrics[metric_name] = float(result[0]['value'][1]) if
                    result else 0
            except Exception as e:
                print(f"Error fetching {metric_name}: {e}")
```

```
                metrics[metric_name] = 0

        return metrics

    def predict_and_store(self, service_name):
        """Generate prediction and store in Elasticsearch"""
        # Fetch metrics
        features = self.fetch_service_metrics(service_name)

        # Format for model
        X = pd.DataFrame([features])

        # Generate prediction
        fault_probability = self.model.predict_proba(X)[0, 1]

        # Update Prometheus metric
        self.prediction_gauge.labels(service=service_name).set(fault_
        probability)

        # Store in Elasticsearch
        doc = {
            'timestamp': datetime.utcnow().isoformat(),
            'service': service_name,
            'fault_probability': fault_probability,
            'metrics': features,
            'model_version': 'v1.2.3',
            'prediction_id': str(uuid.uuid4())
        }

        response = requests.post(
            f'{self.es_host}/fault-predictions/_doc',
            json=doc,
            headers={'Content-Type': 'application/json'}
        )

        return fault_probability
```

```
# Main loop
if __name__ == '__main__':
    engine = FaultPredictionEngine(
        model_path='/models/fault_predictor.pkl',
        prometheus_url='http://prometheus:9090',
        elasticsearch_host='http://elasticsearch:9200'
    )

    services = ['payment-service', 'order-service', 'inventory-service']

    while True:
        for service in services:
            prob = engine.predict_and_store(service)
            print(f"{service}: fault probability = {prob:.3f}")

        time.sleep(60)  # Run predictions every 60 seconds
```

This pipeline runs continuously in Kubernetes, providing real-time fault predictions that influence autoscaling and alerting decisions.

8.7.4 Elasticsearch and Kibana for Observability

Store all prediction results in Elasticsearch with metadata (timestamp, service, fault probability, contributing metrics, model version). Build Kibana dashboards that visualize the following:

- Average fault probability by service over time
- Prediction accuracy compared to actual incidents
- High-risk services exceeding thresholds
- Contributing factors for root cause analysis
- Model performance trends

```
# Create Elasticsearch mapping for predictions
mapping = {
    "properties": {
        "timestamp": {"type": "date"},
```

```
        "service": {"type": "keyword"},
        "fault_probability": {"type": "float"},
        "error_rate": {"type": "float"},
        "latency_p95": {"type": "float"},
        "memory_percent": {"type": "float"},
        "cpu_percent": {"type": "float"},
        "model_version": {"type": "keyword"},
        "prediction_id": {"type": "keyword"}
    }
}

es.indices.put_mapping(index='fault-predictions', body=mapping)
{
  "dashboard": "Fault Prediction Trends",
  "panels": [
    {
      "title": "Average Fault Probability by Service",
      "query": "GET fault-predictions/_search",
      "agg": {
        "terms": {
          "field": "service",
          "avg": {"field": "fault_probability"}
        }
      }
    },
    {
      "title": "Prediction Accuracy Over Time",
      "query": "Comparing predicted faults vs actual incidents"
    },
    {
      "title": "High-Risk Services (>20% fault prob)",
      "query": "fault_probability > 20",
      "size": 100
    }
  ]
}
```

8.8 Validation Strategies for Distributed Fault Prediction

8.8.1 Performance Metrics

Evaluate models using:

- **Precision:** TP/(TP + FP)—Limits false positives disrupting operations
- **Recall (PD):** TP/(TP + FN)—Ensures actual faults are detected early
- **F1 Score:** Harmonic mean balancing precision and recall (target >0.75)
- **AUC-ROC:** Area under ROC curve measures robustness across thresholds
- **Mean time to detection (MTTD):** Quantifies lead time for proactive action

```
def evaluate_model_drift(predictions_df, incidents_df):
    """
    Compare predicted faults against actual incidents to detect model
    degradation

    Args:
        predictions_df: Predictions stored in Elasticsearch
        incidents_df: Actual incidents from incident management system

    Returns:
        Accuracy metrics and drift detection alerts
    """
    # Align predictions with incidents (within 30-minute window before
    incident)
    merged = pd.merge_asof(
        predictions_df.sort_values('timestamp'),
        incidents_df.sort_values('timestamp'),
        on='timestamp',
        by='service',
        direction='backward',
```

```
        tolerance=pd.Timedelta(minutes=30)
    )

    # Calculate weekly accuracy
    merged['week'] = merged['timestamp'].dt.isocalendar().week

    weekly_accuracy = merged.groupby('week').apply(
        lambda x: {
            'precision': precision_score(x['fault'], x['predicted_fault']),
            'recall': recall_score(x['fault'], x['predicted_fault']),
            'f1': f1_score(x['fault'], x['predicted_fault']),
            'auc_roc': roc_auc_score(x['fault'], x['fault_probability'])
        }
    )

    # Alert if accuracy drops >10% from baseline
    baseline_f1 = 0.80
    if weekly_accuracy.iloc[-1]['f1'] < baseline_f1 * 0.9:
        alert(f"Model F1 dropped below threshold: {weekly_accuracy.iloc[-1]
        ['f1']:.3f}")
        return True  # Trigger retraining

    return False
```

8.8.2 A/B Testing in Production

Run controlled experiments with these:

- **Control group:** Deployments without fault prediction
- **Treatment group:** Deployments guided by predictive risk scores and autoscaling

```
# Scheduled retraining job in Kubernetes
apiVersion: batch/v1
kind: CronJob
metadata:
  name: fault-prediction-retrain
spec:
```

```
schedule: "0 2 * * 0"  # Weekly Monday 2 AM
jobTemplate:
  spec:
    template:
      spec:
        containers:
        - name: retrain
          image: fault-predictor-training:latest
          env:
          - name: ELASTICSEARCH_HOST
            value: elasticsearch:9200
          - name: PROMETHEUS_HOST
            value: prometheus:9090
          - name: MODEL_REGISTRY
            value: s3://ml-models
          command:
          - python
          - /scripts/retrain_model.py
        restartPolicy: OnFailure
```

Monitor over several deployment cycles, comparing:

- Mean time between failures (MTBF)
- Mean time to recovery (MTTR)
- Deployment velocity maintained
- Infrastructure cost changes

This validates the operational value of the framework beyond statistical metrics.

8.8.3 Continuous Model Validation and Retraining

The prediction accuracy in microservice environments will decline with time. Introduce a weekly drift-detection check. Issue alerts when the accuracy decreases to a level below 70 percent. Run automated retraining on drift limits.

Adopt a champion/challenger strategy. Compare new models to new models before being completely implemented. Nourish your models with a constant intake of incident data to make them more relevant.

8.8.4 Chaos Engineering Validation

Test frameworks like Gremlin and Chaos Mesh introduce controlled failures and network delays, pod failures, and dependency delays. Make sure that predictions work despite these effects without using services. This bridges the large divide between predictive analytics and resilience engineering.

8.9 Tooling Stack

Automated security scanning and risk measurement through GitHub actions:

- Trivy container vulnerability scanner
- Calculation of Pre-deployment risk score
- Orchestration with deployment
- Artifact creation and implementation through automation

Complicated multi-stage prediction: Use Jenkins:

- Metric aggregation through Elasticsearch
- Build approval gates on a fault-forecasting basis
- View trends in the prediction accuracy dashboard
- Coordination of pipelines at different levels

Kubernetes using KServe/Seldon model serving:

- Implement prediction models as microservices
- Autoscaling inference is load based
- Canary deployments and model versioning
- Quota and isolation of resources

Elastic central observability:

- Metadata index all predictions
- Construct dashboards of fault probability trends
- Set high-risk service alerts
- Create after-incident forensics and root cause analysis

Falco-CrowdStrike integration:

- Detect suspicious containers
- Connect fault prediction to performance anomalies in associates
- Adopt the policy of automated reaction of assaulted containers
- Do data collection for forensic investigations

8.10 Conclusion: Building Predictive Resilience

Microservice architecture fault prediction infrastructure is no monitoring upgrade. It's a predictive resilience strategy facilitator. With observability applied to the DevSecOps pipeline, organizations can avert cascading failures upstream, automate deployments, and improve the integrity of operations.

Fault prediction alters the mode of operation in cloud-native systems, where change is the order of the day. It is not only an increase in availability, but a safer, self-healing infrastructure, which can adapt to the complexity it handles.

The seven steps explained in this chapter based on the organizational needs to continuous validation provide a systematic way to develop and maintain large-scale fault prediction systems. The stages of work are based on the previous ones, forming a feedback mechanism that reinforces predictions in the course of time. Security has been incorporated across the board, as performance enhancements do not create vulnerabilities.

Companies that apply such trends will find that the prediction of faults will be a core infrastructure, and the decision-making process of the development, deployment, and operations teams. The system moves beyond the one-point prediction engine to an organizational capability that works toward the improvement of reliability, security, and speed of deployment nonstop.

CHAPTER 9

Organizational Adoption and Change Management

While the preceding chapters provided the technical structures of isolation, circuit breaking, and anomaly detection, this chapter concentrates on the human and organizational mechanisms that must be in place to enable them. Applying predictive fault detection in the microservices space does not involve installing a tool or two, but rather requires a change a culture. It demands a shift from a reactive position, in which success is whatever it takes to restore a failed system faster, to a proactive position, in which success is whatever it takes to ensure that a system based on self-healing is silent.

The chapter details executive buy-in strategies, engineering team upskilling, trust in probabilistic alerts, and other tangible benefits of predictive DevSecOps.

9.1 Selling Fault Prediction to Stakeholders

Fault prediction may sound to an executive like a costly science project. You need to position predictive DevSecOps as a strategic investment that speeds up delivery and minimizes risks and support this argument with quantifiable results, such as shorter mean time to detect (MTTD) and reduced breach costs.

9.1.1 Business Value Framework

Stakeholders are concerned with three values—speed, stability, and cost. You can respond to these drivers by measuring the benefits (i.e., lower MTTR and proactive vulnerability management) that can reduce the average cost of data breaches (i.e., $4.45 million) by detecting attacks in early stages. Table 9-1 lists these stakeholder concerns and explains how they can be addressed.

D. Sharma and A. Syed, *Fault Detection in Microservice Architectures*,
https://doi.org/10.1007/979-8-8688-2712-9_9

Table 9-1. Address Stakeholder Concerns with Value Propositions

Stakeholder	Core Concern	The "Predictive" Value Proposition
CTO/VP Engineering	Velocity and tech debt	Predictive alerts catch regression bugs before they hit production, reducing rollback rates and freeing up to 20% of senior engineering time currently lost to firefighting.
CFO/Finance	Cost and predictability	Unplanned downtime costs roughly $5,600 per minute. By preempting just four major outages a year, this system pays for itself in Q1.
CISO/Security	Risk and compliance	Anomaly detection identifies security breaches (like data exfiltration) that look like operational faults, catching "low and slow" attacks that static rules miss.
Product Management	User experience	We can detect latency degradation before users complain, preserving our NPS and preventing churn.

You can move beyond simple monitoring by framing the investment as agentic AIOps autonomous systems that detect, decide, and resolve issues without human intervention. This shifts the approach from reactive fixes to proactive prevention, embedding security in every stage for faster time-to-market and lower risks.

9.2 Developer Enablement and Training Practices

It is simple enough to purchase a tool; however, it is difficult to make 500 developers trust it. If the developers don't understand on how the prediction model operates, they will disregard it.

9.2.1 The "Glass Box" Training Curriculum

Training should not just be "how to use the dashboard," but should explain "how the robot thinks." A recommended curriculum includes the following:

1. **Okta basics:<|human|>Introduction to Okta (Week 1)**
    - Normalizing instrumentation using OpenTelemetry.
    - The distinction between sampling (traces) and aggregation (metrics).

2. **Examining probabilistic thinking: (Weeks 3-4)**
   - Shifting binary alerts (disk is full) to probabilistic alert (disk will likely fill in four hours).
   - Learning about confidence intervals. Why an 80 percent confidence warning may be a false positive and how to triage it.
3. **Running feedback loop workshops (ongoing)**
   - **Data load test workshops:** Have teams see the simple statistics of the data of their service. When even a human cannot read the data, then it is too messy to be predicted by AI.
   - **Labeling parties:** Conduct special meetings where experienced engineers discuss historical anomalies and label them (True/False) to retrain the model to create ownership.

9.2.2 Learning Time Allocation

Do not expect adoption by osmosis. Successful organizations allocate dedicated learning time—often a three to six month "ramp-up" period where teams are not penalized for slower feature delivery while they integrate these new practices.

9.3 Overcoming Resistance: Reducing False Positives and Improving Trust

The quickest way to kill a predictive maintenance initiative is alert fatigue. If a developer wakes up at 3 AM for a "predicted failure" that never happens, they will turn off the system.

9.3.1 Strategy 1: The "Shadow Mode" Validation

Never turn on paging for a new predictive model immediately. Run the model in shadow mode for two to four weeks.

- **Action:** The model generates "alerts" into a passive Slack channel or log file, not into PagerDuty.
- **Validation:** Review the channel weekly. Only promote the alert to active paging when it reaches a precision threshold (e.g., >70 percent true positive rate).
- **Psychology:** This proves to the team that the "boy who cried wolf" phase is over before it begins.

9.3.2 Strategy 2: Contextual Anomaly Detection

A basic threshold warning (e.g., CPU > 90 percent) generates false positives when deploying or performing a backup. Use categorical information to provide background.

- **Bad alert:** High latency detected.
- **Good alert:** High latency detected on *Payment Service* specifically for *Version 2.1* in *US-East*, which is anomalous compared to Version 2.0 behavior.
- **Technique:** Use adaptive baselines that learn seasonality (e.g., knowing that traffic spikes on Monday mornings are normal) to reduce false positives from ~20 percent to under 5 percent.

9.3.3 Strategy 3: The "Fallback" Safety Net

Resistance often stems from fear of losing control. Explicitly maintain a "fallback option"—such as access to the old logs or dashboards—so engineers know they can revert to manual debugging if the AI confuses them. This safety net increases their willingness to try the new tool.

9.4 Measuring ROI and Operational Benefits

To justify continued investment, you must measure success. Use a mix of "hard" (financial) and "soft" (cultural) metrics.

9.4.1 Hard Metrics: The Efficiency Dashboard

- **MTTD (mean time to detect):** The most direct measure of predictive success. "Did we find the issue before the customer reported it?"
- **False positive rate (FPR):** Track this ruthlessly. A rising FPR is a leading indicator of tool abandonment.
- **Cost of downtime avoided:** ROI=(Outages Avoided×Avg Cost per Outage).
- **Cost of tooling:** Use the industry benchmark of roughly $5,600/ minute for critical system downtime to build this calculation.

9.4.2 Soft Metrics: The "Burnout" Index

- **On-call sleep quality:** Survey on-call engineers. "How many times were you woken up this month?" A reduction in "zombie alerts" (alerts that require no action) is a huge morale win.
- **Silo unification:** Measure cross-team collaboration. Are the Network and App teams looking at the same predictive dashboard? AIOps often acts as a "single source of truth," forcing siloed teams to agree on what "normal" looks like.

9.5 Creating a Maturity Roadmap for Predictive DevSecOps

Change does not occur at a single instance. Organizations go through a normal sequence of reactive firefighting to self-healing systems. This is a more specific five-stage maturity model based on industry models (CMMI, maintenance maturity models, and SRE practices), which are specifically predictive DevSecOps in microservices architectures.

The roadmap is well balanced with three dimensions—observability/monitoring capabilities, incident response automation, and security integration maturity. Organizations do not often move in a straight line; they can be at Stage 3 of container security and still at Stage 2 of supply chain observability. This hybrid development is natural and anticipated.

9.5.1 Stage 1: Reactive (The "Firefighting" Phase)

Maturity level: Ad hoc, chaotic, crisis-driven operations

Operational Posture

Observability state:

- **Notified on failure only:** "Server Down," "disk Full," "Pod Evicted."
- **Binary alerts:** Do not have confidence scoring or probability reasoning.
- **Logs and metrics:** They are gathered and infrequently actively interrogated.
- **Distributed tracing is nonexistent:** Visibility of the request path is tribal knowledge.
- **Mean MTTD (mean time to detect):** 15-30 minutes (learned very often because of complaints of customers).

Incident response:

- There are no documented runbooks, and all the engineers are ad hoc.
- Controversial paths/directions of escalation; paging is wild and uncontrolled (call whoever knows the system).
- Postmortems are often blame oriented or rare, as opposed to learning oriented.
- No automation of remediation; has to be done manually on every incident.
- Sleep disturbances and burnouts (zombie alerts) of on-call engineers.

Security posture:

- The patches of vulnerability are done manually; scanning is completed before compliance audits.
- No SBOM (Software Bill of Materials) or software supply chain tracking.

- Container images are automatically updated on a regular basis; signature checks are not performed.
- The security groups are not administered ad hoc; the access controls are way too relaxed.
- There is no forecast threat recognition in incident response.

Key Characteristics

- **Downtime cost:** Immeasurable yet catastrophic (average 5,600/ minute to serve critical services)
- **Immediacy of developers:** Blocked by frequent production firefighting; banging of feature work occurs.
- **Compliance posture:** Reactive; SLAs are not real, but are ideals; weeks of manual preparation is audit preparedness.
- **Organizational culture:** No infrastructure to recover quickly and break things.

Actions for Stage 1 Advancement

1. **Establish a baseline instrumentation**
    - Install a central logging system (e.g. ELK, Loki or Grafana).
    - Use OpenTelemetry metrics and traces everywhere.
    - Adopt semantic logging with structured fields (service, version, region, user-tier) so that they can later be correlated.
2. **Measure the current pain**
    - Determine the cost of your three last outages: how long was the downtime × cost/minute?
    - Measure historical incident data/ document MTTR (Mean Time to Repair).
    - Measure toil hours, which are weekly hours spent on routine repetitive incident responses.

3. **Create a minimal runbook template**
    - Use only one runbook format (e.g., Markdown in a Git repo or a wiki). There are sections to be included, such as Symptoms => Detection Strategy => Remediation Steps => Escalation Path.
    - Begin with the three most frequent incidences.
4. **Create a security baseline**
    - Scan all container images in the registry for known CVEs (use Trivy or Grype).
    - Generate a rough SBOM for key services (using Syft or similar).
    - Begin enforcing branch protection rules in version control.

Transition Gate: You're ready for Stage 2 when you have (1) centralized logging/ metrics, (2) documented MTTR baseline, (3) one updated runbook, and (4) a container vulnerability scan report.

9.5.2 Stage 2: Proactive (The "Defined" Phase)

Maturity level: Standardized processes, static thresholds, compliance-driven security

Operational Posture

Observability state:

- Threshold-based notifications are employed instead of binary notifications. CPU greater than 80 percent, Latency greater than 500ms, and error rate greater than 1 percent.
- Alerts are now configured (owner, runbook link, escalation policy) and organized. There are also metrics dashboards that are service specific; developers know how to keep track of their own health.
- Uses distributed tracing (discriminatory on critical paths 5-10 percent) and is discriminative.

Incident response:

- Standardized on-call rotations; escalation paths are documented.
- Runbooks are maintained and linked to alerts; some manual steps are documented.
- Postmortems are scheduled and follow a blameless format.
- Basic runbook automation. Slack notifications and ticket creation, but no auto-remediation.
- Incident templates standardize what information is collected.

Security posture:

- Vulnerability scanning is integrated into CI/CD (SAST, dependency scanning on every build).
- Container images are scanned for CVEs automatically; failing builds block deployment.
- SBOMs are generated at build time (CycloneDX or SPDX format).
- Basic access controls. RBAC in Kubernetes; secrets stored in a vault (HashiCorp Vault, AWS Secrets Manager).
- Supply chain-signed commits and container image signing (using tools like Cosign) are emerging.

Key Characteristics

- **Cost of Downtime:** Quantified and tracked; SLOs are set (e.g., 99.9 percent availability).
- **Developer velocity:** Improved; on-call burden decreased; feature work resumes.
- **Compliance posture:** Audit-ready; SBOM and vulnerability scans are documented; patches follow a defined timeline.
- **Organizational culture:** Move fast and maintain things—stability and velocity are both valued.

Actions for Stage 2 Advancement

1. **Introduce shadow mode for predictive models**
   - Develop a basic anomaly detection model (using statistical methods or simple ML).
   - Generate "predicted alerts" into a passive Slack channel for two to four weeks; do not page.
   - Track the model's precision percent of predictions that are true positives.
   - Only promote to active paging when precision > 70 percent.
2. **Establish seasonality baselines**
   - Collect four to eight weeks of metric data (to capture weekly and daily patterns).
   - Identify "normal" traffic spikes (e.g., Monday mornings, month-end batch jobs).
   - Build contextual baselines, such as "Normal latency for Service A when deployed on Version 2.1 in US-East."
3. **Implement container image signing**
   - Enforce container image signing at build time (using Cosign + OCI Image Spec).
   - Verify signatures at deployment (using admission controllers like Kyverno or OPA/Gatekeeper).
   - Include SBOM in the OCI image artifact.
4. **Use a supply chain: SBOM consumption**
   - Auto-parse SBOMs at deployment; correlate with known vulnerability databases (NVD, GHSA).
   - Create a dashboard, such as the percent of components with known CVEs per service.
   - Define a patch SLA. Critical patches within 24 hours, high patches within one week.

5. **Organize learning sessions**

    - **Conduct a "data load test" workshop:** Show developers their own service's metrics; discuss patterns.
    - **Host a "runbook refinement" meeting:** Do this monthly with on-call engineers and SREs.
    - **Label historical anomalies:** This can include "True outage," "Deployment spike," and "False alarm" to prepare for model training.

Transition Gate: You're ready for Stage 3 when you have (1) a predictive model running in shadow mode with >70 percent precision, (2) seasonality baselines for all critical services, (3) container image signing enforced, (4) SBOM generated and consumable, and (5) monthly training sessions with developer participation.

9.5.3 Stage 3: Predictive (The "Advanced" Phase)

Maturity level: Anomaly-driven alerting, high-confidence automation, behavioral security

Operational Posture

Observability state:

- Anomaly detection replaces static thresholds; alerts warn of *deviations* rather than absolute failures.
- Predictive models run continuously with confidence scores (e.g., "80 percent confident a failure will occur in four hours").
- Alerts include context, such as "Service A latency is 2-sigma above baseline for Version 2.1 in US-East, likely due to X."
- Distributed tracing is comprehensive; all services export traces; sampling is intelligent (error traces at 100 percent , success at 1 percent).
- MTTD <2 minutes; many issues are detected before SLO violation.
- False positive rate <5 percent (down from 20 percent in Stage 2).

Incident response:

- Runbooks are executable; some remediation steps are automated (e.g., "Restart Service," "Scale Pods").
- High-confidence predictions trigger automated remediation; lower-confidence alerts still page humans.
- Confidence thresholds are tuned per alert; critical alerts require >85 percent confidence to auto-act.
- Engineers trust the system; adoption of recommendations is > 80 percent.
- Postmortems now include model performance reviews: "Did the predictor catch this? If not, why?"

Security posture:

- **AI-driven behavioral anomaly detection:** "Service A is talking to Database B for the first time" triggers investigation.
- **Supply chain tracking includes provenance attestations:** "This container was built on 2024-11-30 from Git commit abc123, signed by CI/CD system."
- **Vulnerability remediation is predictive:** Models identify which CVEs will likely be exploited in your specific architecture.
- **Access control is adaptive:** RBAC is combined with anomaly detection (e.g., "User logged in from a new country").
- **Policy-as-code (OPA/gatekeeper):** Enforces compliance rules at admission time.

Key Characteristics

- **Cost of downtime:** Minimized; most incidents are prevented or resolved automatically; unplanned downtime is rare.
- **Developer velocity:** Maximized; on-call is low-stress; engineers spend time on innovation, not firefighting.

- **Compliance posture:** Continuous; audit data is always current; compliance dashboard shows real-time status against NIST, CMMC, or CRA standards.
- **Organizational culture:** Predict and prevent—reliability is a product feature; engineers are empowered to rely on automation.

Actions for Stage 3 Advancement

1. **Migrate alerts to confidence-based triggering**
    - **Redefine alert logic:** "Page if confidence > 80 percent OR if user-facing SLO is already violated."
    - **Introduce "confidence intervals":** Display 50, 80, and 95 percent confidence bounds in dashboards.
    - **Measure FPR (false positive rate):** Do this for each alert type; establish target FPR < 5 percent.
2. **Enable automated remediation for high-confidence predictions**
    - Automated actions for Stage 3: restart pod, scale up, fail over, drain traffic.
    - Require explicit engineer approval for destructive actions (e.g., delete persistent volume).
    - Track "incidents resolved by automation" as a key metric; target >60 percent of recurring incidents.
3. **Implement supply chain provenance tracking**
    - Generate SLSA provenance attestations for all artifacts (container images, binaries).
    - Verify provenance at deployment: "Is this container signed? Does the attestation match our build policies?"
    - Use SBOM + provenance to answer: "Which services are affected by CVE-2024-XYZ?" in < 1 minute.

4. **Implement behavioral security with ML**
    - Train models on "normal" inter-service communication patterns (using distributed traces).
    - Alert on anomalies. New service-to-service connections, unusual data volumes, and abnormal latency.
    - Integrate with automated incident response. Low-confidence anomalies → Slack notification; high-confidence → isolation + alert.
5. **Measure "incidents avoided"**
    - For each predicted incident that auto-remediates, calculate the cost avoided (SLO violation prevented).
    - In the monthly dashboard, add reports, such as "We prevented X incidents costing $Y in downtime."
    - Use this metric in executive reports; tie it to business outcomes.

Transition Gate: You're ready for Stage 4 when you have (1) confidence-based alerts with <5 percent FPR, (2) >60 percent of recurring incidents auto-remediated, (3) SLSA provenance attestations on all artifacts, (4) behavioral anomaly detection running in production, and (5) the "incidents avoided" metric tracked and reported.

9.5.4 Stage 4: Autonomous (The "Agentic" Phase)

Maturity level: Self-healing systems, minimal human intervention, event-driven architecture

Operational Posture

Observability state:

- **Predictive models are deployed as agentic systems:** They observe, decide, and act autonomously.
- **Multi-agent orchestration:** Prediction agent → Decision agent (determine severity) → Remediation agent (execute fix).

- **Observability is self-optimizing:** The system adjusts instrumentation based on recent anomalies.
- **MTTD:** < 30 seconds; most incidents resolve before any human notification.
- **MTTR:** < 1 minute (mostly automated).
- **False positive rate:** < 1 percent; alerts are so reliable that ignoring them is explicitly forbidden.

Incident response:

- Self-healing systems. Kubernetes HPA (Horizontal Pod Autoscaler), circuit breakers, and bulkheads all auto-act.
- Runbooks are fully executable workflows; humans are in the loop only for policy decisions or out-of-bounds scenarios.
- Incident management is mostly observing what the system did; postmortems focus on "why did the system's prediction miss?"
- On-call is fundamentally different: Monitoring for "has the system's self-healing failed?" rather than "is the service up?"

Security posture:

- **Real-time threat blocking:** Predictive models identify attack patterns (e.g., brute-force, data exfiltration) and auto-block.
- **Supply chain:** Agentic systems continuously verify SBOM integrity, provenance, and compliance; noncompliant deployments are prevented.
- **Auto-remediation:** Vulnerable components are automatically patched during maintenance windows; zero-days trigger auto-isolation.
- **Security posture is transparent:** Real-time compliance dashboard shows CMMC/NIST/CRA alignment.

Key Characteristics

- **Cost of downtime:** Near-zero for anticipated failure modes; only novel failures cause SLO violations.
- **Developer velocity:** Unlimited by operational concerns; engineers focus on features, not reliability.
- **Compliance posture:** Continuous and automatic; audits are trivial (system generates reports in real-time).
- **Organizational culture:** The system handles it—operations is a platform, not a team firefighting daily.

Actions for Stage 4 Advancement

1. **Deploy multi-agent orchestration**
    - Implement agentic architecture: Telemetry Agent (collect data) → Prediction Agent (forecast failures) → Decision Agent (evaluate severity + cost) → Remediation Agent (execute fix).
    - Use frameworks like LangChain, AutoGPT, or custom orchestration to coordinate agents.
    - Establish clear handoff points. Each agent passes decision context to the next.
2. **Establish autonomous remediation boundaries**
    - Define a "blast radius" for each auto-remediation action. Which services can auto-restart without human approval?
    - Create a policy layer. Policy-as-code rules that constrain agent actions (e.g., "Never delete a PVC without human approval").
    - Use OPA/Gatekeeper to enforce these policies at runtime.

3. **Implement continuous supply chain verification**
   - **Agentic system continuously monitors:** "Are deployed artifacts still compliant with their SBOMs and provenance?"
   - **Auto-remediation:** Redeploy artifacts with patched dependencies if a vulnerability is detected post-deployment.
   - **Real-time compliance dashboard:** "Percent of production artifacts that pass SLSA Level 3+ verification."
4. **Deploy predictive security threat blocking**
   - ML models trained on attack patterns (brute-force, port scanning, data exfiltration).
   - Real-time anomaly detection in network traffic and application logs.
   - Auto-action. Rate-limit suspicious IPs, revoke user sessions, and trigger security team alerts.
5. **Measure autonomy percentages**
   - **Track:** Percentage of incidents resolved with zero human intervention.
   - **Target:** >95 percent of recurring incidents.
   - **Celebrate:** "Over the past month, the system resolved incidents totaling $X in prevented downtime with zero human interaction."

Transition Gate: You're ready for Stage 5 when you have (1) multi-agent orchestration running in production, (2) >95 percent of incidents resolved autonomously, (3) continuous supply chain verification running, (4) predictive threat blocking active, and (5) exec dashboards showing "autonomous incident resolution ROI."

9.5.5 Stage 5: Mastery (The "Invisible Hand")

Maturity level: Proactive system optimization, continuous learning, competitive advantage

Operational Posture

Observability state:

- Reliability is invisible to end users. Incidents are so rare they become news ("The incident of Q4 2024").
- Predictive accuracy is >99 percent on known failure modes; only novel attack vectors cause issues.
- The system learns from every incident. Model retraining happens automatically post-remediation.
- The error budget is a resource to be used strategically (e.g., "We have 43 hours of downtime budget this quarter; let's use it for a controlled chaos experiment.").
- Observability itself is continuously optimized. The system adds/ removes instrumentation based on relevance.

Incident response:

- When incidents occur, they resolve within SLA automatically; human involvement is rare.
- The incident becomes a learning opportunity. ML models are retrained; policies are refined; and edge cases are covered.
- On-call has shifted to "innovation on-call." Engineers spend time on experiments, not alerts.

Security posture:

- **Security is proactive:** Threat models evolve; attacks are predicted before they manifest.
- **Supply chain security:** Compliance is continuous; audits are formalities ("the system passed compliance checks 10,000 times this year").
- **Zero-trust architecture is native:** Every request is verified against real-time threat models.

Key Characteristics

- **Cost of downtime:** Measured in fractions; competitive advantage is now resilience.
- **Developer velocity:** Constrained only by imagination and resources, not operational concerns.
- **Compliance posture:** Automated and continuous; zero audit surprises.
- **Organizational culture:** Reliability is built in—operations is a solved problem; strategic focus shifts to scaling innovation.

Actions for Stage 5 Advancement

1. **Continuous model optimization**
    - Implement continuous learning. After each incident is resolved, retrain prediction models.
    - A/B test remediation strategies; use reinforcement learning to optimize remediation workflows.
    - Ensemble models. Combine multiple prediction models for higher accuracy.
2. **Chaos engineering as a compliance tool**
    - Run scheduled chaos experiments. "Break this service in a controlled way; verify auto-remediation."
    - Use results to refine predictions and remediation actions.
    - Make chaos engineering part of the release process for critical services.
3. **Supply chain attestation chains**
    - Track full lineage: Source code → Build → Artifact → Deployment → Runtime.
    - Use SBOM + provenance + runtime telemetry to create a "trust score" for each artifact.
    - Automatically rotate or isolate low-trust artifacts.

4. **Cross-organizational security intelligence sharing**
    - Participate in threat intelligence sharing (e.g., STIX/TAXII feeds).
    - Use industry-wide threat data to improve your predictive threat models.
    - Publish anonymized incident patterns to the community.
5. **Measure your competitive advantage**
    - **Calculate:** "What percent of our uptime comes from autonomous prevention vs. fast response?"
    - **Compare against industry benchmarks:** "Our MTTR is 10x faster than competitors; this saves us $X in revenue."
    - **Use maturity as a sales/marketing tool:** "We operate at Stage 5 DevSecOps maturity; here's the proof."

9.6 Cross-Cutting Concerns: Advancing All Dimensions

No organization advances uniformly. However, these cross-cutting practices accelerate progress across all stages, as shown in Table 9-2.

Table 9-2. *Organizational Change Management*

Stage	Focus	Action
Stage 1-2	Build trust in automation	Run "shadow mode" pilots; celebrate small wins
Stage 2-3	Shift culture from "heroes fix things" to "systems prevent things"	Reward prevention; track "incidents avoided" in performance reviews
Stage 3-4	Empower autonomous systems	Establish clear policy boundaries; remove approval bottlenecks for auto-remediation
Stage 4-5	Measure competitive advantage	Create executive dashboards showing downtime avoided, compliance automation ROI

9.6.1 Data Quality

Prediction accuracy is bounded by data quality. Use this progression:

- **Stage 1:** Raw logs; high noise; many false signals.
- **Stage 2:** Structured logs with semantic fields; correlation possible.
- **Stage 3:** Cleaned, normalized telemetry; ML models are useful.
- **Stage 4:** High-fidelity telemetry; models are highly accurate.
- **Stage 5:** Telemetry is optimized for prediction; only signal is collected.

9.6.2 Policy-as-Code Evolution

- **Stage 1:** No policies; ad hoc decisions.
- **Stage 2:** Basic policies (e.g., "no public S3 buckets"); enforced through code review.
- **Stage 3:** Automated policy enforcement (OPA/Gatekeeper); policies embedded in CI/CD.
- **Stage 4:** Adaptive policies; policies change based on threat model.
- **Stage 5:** Policies are auto-generated; a policy engine learns which governance rules are optimal.

Table 9-3 shows how supply chain maturity is aligned with CISA and NIST SSDF.

Table 9-3. *Supply Chain Maturity (Aligned with CISA and NIST SSDF)*

Stage	SBOM	Provenance	Vulnerability Management
Stage 1	None	Ad hoc; manual tracking	Reactive; scanned before audits
Stage 2	Generated at build time (CycloneDX); static	Commits signed; images signed	Scanned in CI/CD; patching on schedule
Stage 3	Generated and validated; consumed at deployment	Attestations included in OCI artifacts	Predictive: "which CVEs matter for us?"
Stage 4	SBOM is continuously verified; VEX (Vulnerability Exploitability Exchange) data included	Real-time verification; noncompliant artifacts auto-isolated	Auto-patching during maintenance windows
Stage 5	SBOM is part of a continuous supply chain graph	Trustworthiness scoring based on full lineage	Zero-days auto-isolated; patches deployed faster than disclosure

9.7 Conclusion: The Maturity Roadmap in Practice

9.7.1 Quick Stage Assessment

Answer these questions to assess your organization's current stage:

1. **How long does it take to detect an issue? (MTTD)**
    - 15-30 min → Stage 1
    - 3-10 min → Stage 2
    - <2 min → Stage 3
    - <30 sec → Stage 4
    - <10 sec (mostly prevented) → Stage 5

2. **What percent of incidents resolve without human intervention?**
    - <5% → Stage 1
    - 5-20% → Stage 2
    - 20-60% → Stage 3
    - 60-95% → Stage 4
    - 95% → Stage 5
3. **How is your alert precision?**
    - 20% false positives → Stage 1
    - 5-20% → Stage 2
    - <5% → Stage 3
    - <1% → Stage 4
    - 99% accuracy → Stage 5
4. **What is your SBOM + Provenance status?**
    - None → Stage 1
    - Generated but not consumed → Stage 2
    - Validated at deployment → Stage 3
    - Continuously verified post-deployment → Stage 4
    - Part of real-time trust scoring → Stage 5

9.7.2 The Change Leader's Checklist

- **Identify the why:** Determine the cost of the three previous outages. Introduce executives to this number.
- **Secure the team:** Implement a policy of shadow modes on any new alerts; do not page unless precision is over 70 percent.

- **Train the intuition:** Conduct a regular (e.g., monthly) workshop on data load; demonstrate to devs the metrics and trends of their own service.
- **Measure the silence:** Report on "incidents avoided" not just "incidents fixed." Make prevention visible.
- **Celebrate progress:** Each stage advancement is worth celebrating; tie it to team OKRs and individual performance.
- **Iterate on policy:** Every six months, review automation boundaries; push policies to be more permissive as trust grows.
- **Market the supply chain as a competitive edge:** By Stage 4+, your supply chain security is a differentiator; market it to customers.

PART V

Future Outlook

CHAPTER 10

Conclusion and Future Outlook

10.1 Recap of Key Methodologies and Findings

In this technical exploration, we have determined that predictive fault detection represents a paradigm shift in the approach of organizing system reliability in DevSecOps environments. The human path to the conditions of the active response to reactive incidents and the active prevention of failures both require an in-depth study of various interrelated fields—distributed system architecture, development of machine learning models, operational resilience patterns, and organizational maturation of capabilities.

The fundamental methodologies studied throughout this book demonstrate a number of universal facts that are not limited to cases of implementation. To begin with, hybrid AI models, which include several machine learning methods, are always highly effective at detecting anomalies, time-series, reinforcement learning, and statistical models than the separate applications of the individual methods. In 2024-2025, researchers showed that systems that use XGBoost and LightGBM to predict fault in the initial stages of operation have a higher accuracy-recall ratio than single-based neural networks. Implementations based on the ensemble techniques lower the false positives and do not decrease the sensitivity to true signals of failure.

Second, the system patterns in which these systems are implemented are significant. The Sidecar pattern deployment has 76.5 percent effectiveness rates and relative low overheads (4-7 percent) and orchestration framework integration has 89 percent effectiveness to infrastructure-level failures and average recovery durations of 31.5

D. Sharma and A. Syed, *Fault Detection in Microservice Architectures*,
https://doi.org/10.1007/979-8-8688-2712-9_10

seconds, which is orders of magnitude faster than manual intervention cycles with an average of 10.2 minutes. These are not just minor upgrades—these are the difference between having service and an infrastructure failure that spills over.

Thirdly, observability and data quality are the two cornerstones to a successful predictive system. Typical starting deployments perform at 70-75 percent accuracy, and the improvement curve continues over three to six months as deployments learn through corrected predictions and increased thresholds. Organizations that invested in detailed distributed tracing (through either OpenTelemetry or Jaeger), standard metrics gathering in the cloud-native ecosystem, and standard logging structures model improvement rates were 40 times faster than those without instrumentation.

The most notable observation in the context of real-world deployments is the paramount role that model drift and data quality take in a systematic way. The data in production systems is constantly changing due to fluctuating user patterns and infrastructure development as well as operational contexts. Historical pattern-trained models perform worse on data distributions that are dissimilar enough to the training patterns. In fact, recorded results indicate that accuracy deteriorates as much as 94 percent to 46 percent as deployment conditions diverge completely upon training conditions.

10.2 From Research to Real-World Adoption: Lessons Learned

The move between scholarly prototypes and tightly regulated pilot scenarios to at-scale deployments has surfaced lessons to be learned and critical changes to make.

10.2.1 The False Positive Paradox

Probably the most important implication is that minimizing false positives cannot be an after-thought. It must be part of the initial design of models and maintained throughout the system's lifecycle. Organizations that optimized false positive reduction had 40-50 percent lower total cost of ownership than those that optimized raw sensitivity. This is due to the fact that every false alarm causes an operational overhead cost: engineers investigate non-problems, divert focus on actual problems, and suffer decision fatigue, which ultimately desensitizes the teams to all alerts. False alarms cost structure is so inherently asymmetric. The single false maintenance alert to an organization does not only entail direct costs involved in service intervention, but opportunity cost, which is the failure to service the scheduled maintenance windows, misallocation of resources, and worst of all, loss of trust in automated systems. In cases where the false alarm rate goes above 30 percent of the total alerts, studies have indicated that teams start to ignore the alerting system altogether and go back to the reactive firefighting mode. Practitioners should aim for false positives less than 15 percent as the minimum to production deployment and mature systems should be less than 8 percent. This involves making investments in decision structure that include contextual reasoning and multi-signal correlation rather than threshold tuning on individual measures.

10.2.2 The Data Quality Investment

Organizations that prioritized data quality issues as a secondary consideration were faced with delays of 18-24 months before reaching a target performance measure. On the other hand, teams that invested in data cleaning, feature engineering, and retrospective labeling of past incidents recorded production readiness within six to nine months. This is not an issue of complexities, but where it is front-loaded at a time when it can be of maximum benefit.

Some critical data quality efforts are setting up ground truth labeling schemes with more than one independent labeler (noise in labels reduces model generalization); continuous data quality monitoring to support schema change or distribution shifts; creating a complete data dictionary to standardize measures of concepts used by different teams; and retaining historical data over a period of 12-24 months to facilitate strong retraining of models. The best-performing systems in these organizations customarily allocated 40-50 percent of overall effort to data management, 30-35 percent to model development, and 15-25 percent to operational integration and monitoring. This is an allocation that goes against intuitive expectations, but is important when in a production environment.

10.2.3 Human-in-the-Loop as a Strategic Necessity

It has been theorized that autonomous self-healing systems are the final stage in the maturity of predictive fault detection. Patterns of deployment in the real world are different. Most effective production implementations have adopted a degree of autonomy in which mundane and low-risk problems will initiate full automation of the remedies, whereas complex situations or high-stakes decisions will retain human control. Literature records that 83 percent of successful autonomous remediation applications use of this hybrid method. The major point is that the level of trust regarding automation should not be forced but rather achieved in the process of its performance.

Organizations that entered with human-approval workflows to all of the remediation actions, slowly increasing automation to categories of exceptional accuracy and low-consequence impact, had 60-70 percent faster organizational adoption than those that tried to do full automation at once. The second important use of human-in-the-loop systems is that they offer a way of providing continuous feedback loops in order to improve models. Once human beings are validating, overriding, or correcting automated decisions, such indications supply precious training data in the next version of the model. Companies that completed this feedback loop in an orderly fashion realized 15 percent higher rates of success in the remediation process in the first six months of operation, which is significantly better than those that treated the human input as a crutch that would be dislodged after a few months.

10.2.4 Cross-Functional Collaboration as a Infrastructure Requirement

DevSecOps maturity models recognize that people and culture is a baseline requirement, but most organizations do not fully appreciate the investment that needs to be made to operationalize this as an aspirational objective. Siloed teams cannot be used successfully in predictive fault detection. The security architect of the model attack surface should coordinate with platform engineers working on observability infrastructure, developers working on deployment automation, and operations people working on incident response processes. Organizations that define formal cross-functional governance practices, weekly architecture review meetings, share OKRs across both development and operations, and share incident perspectives involving representation across all functional areas reported 30-40x faster feature development as well as 25x fewer production incidents than organizations that relied on informal collaboration.

The trend that was taking shape remained the same: collaboration structures should be formalized, measured, and reinforced constantly. DevSecOps teams following metrics such as time to issue recognition to cross-functional resolution of problems and percentage of critical decisions based on all stakeholder representation stayed engaged and did not tend to backslide to past silos.

10.2.5 Organizational Readiness Assessment

Implementation timelines correlate strongly with organizational DevSecOps maturity at project initiation. Teams beginning at "Intermediate" DevSecOps maturity (established CI/CD pipelines, basic security testing, cross-functional communication) typically require six to nine months to production deployment. Those beginning at "Beginner" maturity frequently need 18-24 months, with extended timelines driven by foundational capability gaps rather than technical complexity.

10.3 The Evolving Role of Predictive Fault Detection in DevSecOps

Predictive fault detection is not a fixed technical approach, but a dynamic capability, and it will always have to adapt to the evolving threat environment, new architectures, and company priorities.

10.3.1 From Infrastructure to Supply Chain Resilience

DevSecOps has grown exponentially to the point where the whole software supply chain is included, not only runtime infrastructure but model artifacts, build dependencies, container images, and AI-produced pieces of code. The predictive fault detection should also change to accommodate failures that occur along this very long supply chain.

Recent studies prove the fact that supply chain vulnerabilities are now the attack vectors on the same level as the runtime exploits. Companies that have integrated AI models based on threat information that encompasses attacks targeting supply chains have been reported to respond 28 times faster and have a recovery time 19 times shorter than manual contingency management. All these changes will necessitate predictive systems that are made to encompass supply chain observability and infrastructure monitoring: tracing model lineage and integrity, tracking dependency freshness and vulnerability status, and certifying artifact provenance and signatures. The intersection of fault detection and supply chain security results in the development of novel architectural patterns. Federated learning strategies allow companies to cooperatively identify anomaly detectors among ecosystem participants without storing sensitive operation data in one place. This method takes into consideration two concerns at the same time: enhancing the generalization of models using aggregated data and preserving privacy of data using decentralized structures. Initial applications indicate a 17-35 percent reduction in aggregation latency and communication overhead relative to classic centralized methodologies.

10.3.2 Agentic AI as an Emerging Complexity Layer

The appearance of autonomous AI agents presents completely novel failure modes that cannot be managed by traditional predictive systems. In contrast to deterministic applications, agentic systems are non-deterministic: agents are autonomous, their decision-making is fluid with respect to interactions, and they have memory that enables them to modify their strategies over time depending on the dynamics.

These attributes necessitate predictive fault-detection systems that transform past binary failure/success identification into constant behavior anomaly identification. The technical difficulty is complicated by the security issues. Research suggests that agentic AI systems are susceptible to different attack vectors:

- Prompt injection attacks, which modify agent instructions
- Model poisoning, which distorts learned agent behavior
- Memory tampering, which introduces false information into the agent context
- Cascading failure attacks, where entities compromised by attacks spread the attack through agent networks

An agentic environment predictor needs real-time behavioral baselines that represent the normal behavioral patterns of agents (frequency of API calls, data access volumes, inter-system communication streams). The model must be continually updated to reflect actual behavioral changes versus malicious changes. Agentic AI also needs a mechanism of responding that can mitigate a system without impacting the system on a larger scale. Companies with agentic AI security viewed as a separate incident response tier have responded to incidents 40x faster than those that used legacy security measures.

10.3.3 Integration with Compliance and Risk Quantification

The sphere of modern DevSecOps functions in more complicated regulatory environments—CRA (Cyber Resilience Act), RED EN 18031, NIST AI Risk Management Framework, and industry-related demands. Compliance requirements should not be added later, as predictive fault-detection systems need to be designed with them in mind at the beginning of the architecture. This involves measuring cyber risk in a manner that will be attractive to business stakeholders and compliance systems. Graph-based supply chain structure analysis algorithms can identify critical dependencies that are overburdened by organizational resilience. According to the Gartner 2025 Resilience Benchmark data, organizations that applied risk-sensitive metrics using AI models reported significantly better recovery times. The trick here is to translate technical metrics (MTTD, MTTR, false positive rates) into information that is relevant to the business (recovery time in minutes, cost per incident avoided, compliance attestation automation).

10.4 Open Research Areas: AI-Driven Automation, Supply Chain Resilience

Significant opportunities remain for advancing technical capability and organizational practice in predictive fault detection and DevSecOps integration.

10.4.1 Model Accuracy Under Distribution Shift

Although present-day implementations are highly accurate in a controlled laboratory environment, the performance of production drops significantly when the circumstances of the operation do not correspond to the training situations. The research area has no established methods to: (1) dynamically identify the presence of a distribution shift without ground truths, (2) handle continuous distribution change sin a model, (3) trade off retraining frequency with computational cost, and (4) graciously degrade across multiple generations of infrastructure.

Future research directions should focus on creating principled methods of concept drift mitigation that perform well in resource-constrained edge networks, devising techniques of transfer learning by training models on one topology and deploying them to newer networks, and exploring methods of online learning that can continuously adapt without necessarily retraining their entire model. To identify a distribution shift, organizations that adopt predictive systems need to watch leading indicators of possible distribution shift; the development of clusters of prediction failures on subsets of infrastructure; developing patterns of prediction failures; and inconsistencies between predicted and observed patterns of failures. This is achieved by having automatic retraining pipelines activated by these signs instead of a predetermined schedule to ensure a more efficient model performance.

10.4.2 Hybrid Human-AI Decision-Making Under Uncertainty

The existing methods consider the human control as a transitional necessity that should be reduced to a minimum. Instead, research should examine the optimal way to organize human-AI collaboration in cases where humans and algorithms are complementary. Humans are good at contextual reasoning, identifying new patterns of failures, and high-consequence trade-off decisions. Algorithms are best at scale processing sensor data of high dimensionality, finding statistical patterns in large-scale data, and consistent decisions of scale. It is probable that optimal systems will have different structures of decision-making, depending on the severity of consequences, with low-consequence, high-confidence decisions being completely automated; moderate-consequence decisions involving contextual presentation of recommendations; and high-consequence decisions starting with systematic human review and algorithmic decision support. Research is needed on (1) defining the levels of consequences by category of different types of failures and remediation, (2) the interface design to show algorithmic reasoning on human beings, and (3) human trust calibration and performance degradation metrics under various information presentation strategies.

10.4.3 Supply Chain Resilience Through Federated Intelligence

The new attack space that involves model dependencies, data provenance, and artifact integrity opens up new resilience strategies. Federated learning across distributed ecosystems allows organizations to work together to enhance anomaly detection without hosting operation telemetry, which is sensitive. Areas of research interest comprise the following:

- The design of effective aggregation strategies that minimize communication overhead in geographically dispersed environments
- The design of mechanisms that enable heterogeneous participants (organizations of various sizes, sectors, maturity levels) to add value to shared models
- The design of protocols to trust in federated environments where the participants are unable to audit all participation
- The design of incentive mechanisms that allow heterogeneous parties to take part in collaborative security initiatives in a meaningful way.

Federated learning is an area of study that should be initiated by large organizations that have supplier ecosystems in their industry consortia. First, non-sensitive use cases (macro infrastructure patterns, aggregate failure rates) must be initially attempted before moving on to sensitive areas.

10.4.4 Autonomous Recovery in Complex Distributed Systems

Disaster recovery in self-healing has come to a new level of maturity when it comes to infrastructure-level problems (pod restarts, replica adjustments). However, application-level recovery of failures is highly manual or uses scripted workflows that are fragile. The following should be investigated:

- Automated root cause analysis that does not just correlate but tries to infer the underlying cause of failure within service dependency chains

- Selection of remediation strategies that consider the impact down a chain of service dependencies
- Recovery validation that can assert that values have been recovered without long-term observation

The situation becomes even more problematic when multi-region deployments, state consistency requirements, and cascading failure scenarios are considered. The new methods (based on the reinforcement learning) promise a learning agent that learns the effectiveness of remediation strategies through interactions with simulated failure states, where recovery time is minimized and service disruption is minimized. Full rollouts of RL-based recovery had a 15 percent higher success rate when implemented maturely than when it was first used in half a year.

10.5 Final Recommendations for Practitioners and Researchers

10.5.1 For Security Architects and DevSecOps Leaders

Establish Foundational Infrastructure Before Deploying Predictive Systems

Predictive fault detection cannot be made to work as a point solution overlayed on an underdeveloped infrastructure. To have a foundation that is healthy, organizations need to make sure that their foundation has the following: a cohesive observability across logs, metrics and traces; standardized incident response processes with well-defined escalation protocols; cross-functional governance designs with established decision making authority; and a formal DevSecOps capability evaluation that reflects at least Intermediate maturity.

Prioritize False Positive Minimization from Project Inception

In contrast to the conventional machine learning problems, where high sensitivity is an important feature, operational fault-detection systems should be a balance to sensitivity and false positive cost. Have hard targets in terms of false positive rates (below 15 percent for initial deployments, below 8 percent for mature systems) and do not use these as a secondary measure. Invest in advanced decision frameworks with contextual reasoning, multi-signal correlation, and staged alerting. Show uncertain predictions as recommendations, not as hard and fast alarms.

Design Human-in-the-Loop from the Beginning, Not as a Retrofit

The autonomous remediation, instead, should be seen as an evolution, rather than revolution. Start with human approval needed in all remediation efforts, creation of performance baselines, and creation of organizational trust. Ongoingly increase automation to certain categories of actions that are exceptional in terms of accuracy and low consequence effects. Use human decisions as useful feedback and complete the loop to keep on improving the performance of the model.

Implement Comprehensive Change Management and Organizational Readiness Programs

Technical implementation is just 20-30 percent of the effort in terms of the successful predictive fault-detection programs. Invest equal resources in: change management to deal with the changes in team roles; communications program to clarify what the system can or cannot do; skill training to ensure that operations staff are capable of processing and acting on systemic advice; and culture transformation to reenforce a spirit of collective accountability toward system resilience.

Measure and Track Business Outcomes, Not Just Technical Metrics

MTTD and MTTR are helpful in terms of operational understanding. Convey value through business-oriented measures: cost per avoided incident, revenue safeguard due to prevented outages, compliance standards automated, and risk quantification enhancements. Companies that monitor business performance receive a lot more stakeholder interest to proceed with investment.

10.5.2 For Researchers and Academic Communities

Develop Robust Model Adaptation Techniques for Production Environments

Existing scholarly sources are more concerned with one-time model training and deployment. The real-world systems are in need of constant changes as the environments change. Accent in research should focus on: (1) principled methods of detecting concept drift that can be performed without the use of ground truth signals, (2) effective retraining methods based on trade-offs between performance improvement and computational cost, (3) transfer learning methods based on the use of models across infrastructure topologies, and (4) online learning methods that support the ongoing evolution of models.

Create Evaluation Frameworks Reflecting Production Realities

Academic benchmarking tends to use fixed sets of data and single metrics (accuracy, precision, recall) that are not reflective of production issues. Create assessment systems that use distribution shift cases, computational resource constraints, false positive cost asymmetry, model drift with long periods of deployment, and patterns of human-AI interactions. Benchmark systems should make longitudinal datasets available so that researchers can study model degradation patterns and recovery patterns over realistic time durations (6-24 months).

Investigate Optimal Human-AI Collaboration Structures

The human oversight is seen in literature as a constraint that has to be broken instead of an appreciable aspect of resilient systems. Study how best to design decisions according to the severity of the consequences involved, the interface design that effectively conveys the algorithmic reasoning, the human trust calibration to various information presentation strategies, and the organizational learning based on human correction and overrides.

Pursue Federated Learning for Ecosystem-Scale Resilience

The concept of supply chain security is currently demanding distributed intelligence by more than one organization. Future research should focus on: (1) aggregation techniques to minimize communication overhead, (2) schemes to allow the contribution of meaning by heterogeneous participants, (3) trust protocols when meaningful contribution by participants cannot be fully audited, and (4) incentive schemes to make collaboration in security worthwhile.

Develop Causal Inference Techniques for Root Cause Analysis

Whereas correlation-based anomaly detection has become sufficiently mature, production systems require causal knowledge. Not that failures have happened, but why, in the chains of dependency of services. Causal inference research on distributed systems would potentially significantly enhance the accuracy of remediation and allow solutions to be developed that deal with root causes and not the symptoms.

10.5.3 For Enterprise Technology Leaders

Establish Predictive Fault Detection as a Strategic Initiative, Not a Tactical Tool

Organizations that try to implement predictive systems without executive support and cross-functional governance are unlikely to be successful in the long term. Make this ability strategic, use multi-year budgets (rather than project-related appropriations), and entrench predictive resiliency into organizational KPIs and compensation systems.

Build Supply Chain Observability Commensurate with Direct Operations Observability

With the growth of software supply chains (including pre-trained models, adapters, plugins, and third-party dependencies), there is a corresponding growth in observability that needs to be adopted. Invest in Software Bill of Materials (SBOM) generation and tracking, artifact provenance verification, model integrity attestation, and dependency vulnerability monitoring. It is only through this end-to-end visibility that predictive systems can operate efficiently in the whole value delivery chain.

Develop Organizational Competency in Model Operations and MLOps

Predictive systems need specialized operational skills that are not like traditional infrastructure operations. Data engineering and quality assurance, model performance monitoring and retraining, feature engineering and selection, and continuous model validation should be assigned specific positions in organizations. This understanding recognizes the fact that machine learning systems are fundamentally different to manage in the same way that deterministic software is.

Create Feedback Loops Between Operations and Development Through Predictive Systems

DevSecOps works when the development and operations teams have visibility of the system behavior and work together in the continuous improvement process. Predictive fault-detection systems provide natural feedback. The context of an incident is available through operations, and the results of a remediation are available through the operations, which can be used to make better future models; development takes the insights provided by operations to make architectural improvements. These feedback systems should be formalized by the organization in terms of joint reviews, common measures, and congruent incentive systems.

10.6 Conclusion: The Path Forward

Predictive fault detection represents a fundamental capability for organizations operating complex, distributed systems at production scale. The journey from research prototypes to operational systems requires simultaneous advancement across multiple dimensions, technical sophistication in machine learning and systems design, organizational maturity in cross-functional collaboration, and strategic commitment to resilience as a core business value.

Organizations that will thrive in increasingly complex technology landscapes are those that treat predictive resilience not as a feature to be added, but as a foundational capability to be cultivated. This requires upfront investment in observability infrastructure, data quality, organizational readiness, and human-AI collaboration structures. The investment proves worthwhile. Mature predictive systems reduce mean time to recovery by orders of magnitude, prevent catastrophic cascading failures, and transform operations from reactive firefighting to proactive optimization.

The field remains immature in several dimensions. Research continues to refine model accuracy under distribution shift, develop techniques for autonomous recovery in complex systems, and investigate optimal human-AI collaboration. Organizations deploying predictive systems today serve as both practitioners executing current best practices and researchers contributing to collective knowledge about what works in production environments.

The future evolution of predictive fault detection within DevSecOps will be shaped by several trends: expanding scope to encompass supply chain resilience alongside infrastructure monitoring, incorporation of agentic AI as autonomous decision-makers require new anomaly detection approaches, integration with compliance and risk quantification frameworks as regulatory complexity intensifies, and deepening human-AI collaboration as we move beyond the false choice between full automation and manual operations.

Organizations investing now in predictive capabilities position themselves to lead this evolution, learning from early experience and contributing to industry knowledge. Those deferring this investment risk falling behind, facing increasingly severe operational and competitive consequences as system complexity continues to accelerate. The path forward is clear: thoughtful, measured, human-centered adoption of predictive fault detection as a strategic differentiator in organizational DevSecOps maturity.

Index

D. Sharma and A. Syed, *Fault Detection in Microservice Architectures*,
https://doi.org/10.1007/979-8-8688-2712-9

D

E

F

G

H

I

N

O

P, Q

R

S

T

U

V

W

X, Y

Z

GPSR Compliance
The European Union's (EU) General Product Safety Regulation (GPSR) is a set of rules that requires consumer products to be safe and our obligations to ensure this.

If you have any concerns about our products, you can contact us on

ProductSafety@springernature.com

In case Publisher is established outside the EU, the EU authorized representative is:

Springer Nature Customer Service Center GmbH
Europaplatz 3
69115 Heidelberg, Germany

www.ingramcontent.com/pod-product-compliance
Lightning Source LLC
Chambersburg PA
CBHW081251130726
47998CB00010B/2751
9798868827112